# Running with Razors and Soul

## A Handbook for Competitive Runners

# Running with Razors and Soul

## A Handbook for Competitive Runners

## G. Kent

*Bandit Press*

ISBN-10: 0615768709
ISBN-13: 978-0615768700
LCCN: 2013903187

This book is dedicated to:

Coach Giles Godfrey – Granada Hills High School
Cross Country Coach
Coach Pat Connolly – Coach/Founder Encino
Track Club
Coach Kurt Nelson – California Lutheran
University Cross Country Coach

And:

Bob and Jim Evans, Keith Cooney, Mark Haberer, Bill King, Mike Lampson, Mike Newman, Paul Burch, Alan Silver, Tom Horton, Mike Baker, Steve Appleby, Don Bogle, Ken Long, Merle and Les Fleming, Richard Little, Brian Carroll, Bob Burns, Chuck and Greg Franklin, Jim Hanifan, Kim and Kerry Ellison, Gary Mazziotti, Scott Skelton, Jim Bostwick, Chuck LaGamma, Warren Kumley, George Fotinakes, and Richard Knapp

# CONTENTS

# Foreword

*"Rewardful afternoons for tired winners."*
                                    –Jack Kerouac

    G. Kent's new book, *Running with Razors and Soul,* will motivate and encourage the most elite runner as well as the average jogger. The book inspires a new type of mental determination that can benefit runners at all levels. Kent's anecdotal style and tough but nurturing tone will help improve any runner who possesses the courage and commitment to rise above the challenges that the sport entails.

    At the beginning of the 2009 cross country season, I read chapters from *Running with Razors and Soul* to my team at Villages High School in central Florida. My team benefitted from the wisdom of Kent's running experiences and internalized his ideas as the season progressed. Before my team began its Monday workouts, I read the chapter "Belief" in order to instill confidence and initiate a new attitude through rigorous mental and physical training. This new mindset led our team to the State meet in Dade City, Florida in mid-November.

    As we climbed off the bus at the State meet for the first time in our school's history, I used a direct quote from the book about "using your future suffering" to help motivate them for their upcoming race. I know this statement sounds like a paradox, but my team of seven gangly, committed young men knew exactly what Kent was preaching from that chapter in *Running with Razors and Soul*. They approached the starting line at the State Championship with a "sharpened edge of competitive toughness, physical and mental, and demonstrated the heart and desire to run with no limitations."

As a result, a special group of guys, with support from their parents, friends, coaches and Kent's book, ran to a tenth place finish out of twenty-five teams. It was a joy to watch the expressions on their fatigued faces when the results were announced. Each boy realized that by "running with razors and soul" he had achieved the greatest cross country season in school history. To each runner, Kent's book was more than a running manual, it was a way of life. This is a book that will challenge, motivate and benefit any runner who reads it.

Keith E. Baumann
Villages High School
The Villages, Florida

# The Old Runner

the old distance runner
eases out

settles into his pace

hears the creek flow
feels the wind blow
sees the sun shine
knows his right mind

he's old and slow
but he can still go

he stretches before and after

he drinks a lot of water

-    **Daniel Barth**

# PROLOGUE

*"…and I knew what the loneliness of the long distance runner running across the country felt like, realizing that as far as I was concerned this feeling was the only honesty and realness there was in the world."*

> –Alan Sillitoe,
> *The Loneliness of the Long Distance Runner*

Midway through my 1966 senior cross country campaign at Granada Hills High School in Los Angeles, I approached Coach Giles Godfrey in his gymnasium office with a personal matter. The room was cluttered with trophies, photos and news clippings attesting to the ten L.A. City Championships his cross country teams had captured.

"May I have a word, Coach?"

"Come in, Kent," he growled from behind his desk, "and shut the damn door."

Our discussion followed the cross country team's weekly Friday afternoon "death march" across the foothills below Mission Peak, the San Fernando Valley's most northern and prominent landmark. The Granada Hills High School training area encompassed over one hundred miles of dirt roads and trails, located in a lush setting that included steep ravines with seasonal creeks and groves of cottonwoods and eucalyptus. The roads and trails were scented with mint, sage and nettles that intensified during the torrid September/October dog days of the season. The cross country team shared the acreage with no one, courtesy of the J. Paul Getty Oil Company, whose management professed to be fans of the long distance runner. At least that's how Coach Godfrey explained his success in procuring our special privileges to climb over locked gates and ignore No Trespassing signs, while running the hills with coyote, rabbit, rattlesnake, mountain lion and an occasional oil derrick.

Thursdays were our scheduled "meet days" at Pierce College, and the day before had witnessed the dismantling of Monroe High School by a score of 15-36. (In cross country 15 is a shutout.) Every Friday we endured Godfrey's infamous seventeen-mile course. The junior varsity and tenth grade teams completed an abbreviated twelve-mile version, but the varsity ran the entire distance. Our routine consisted of three miles to loosen up, twelve leisurely miles to a locked gate near Stoney Point, and then an all-out race the final two miles back to Granada Hills High School.

Coach Godfrey motioned for me to sit. "Well, speak up."

I said, "Coach, my problem is that every week during the pre-race warm-ups, the varsity follow me around like a flock of baby ducks. They mimic my every move."

"So?"

"Oxygen," I cried. "I need my space in order to get mentally prepared. My concentration is totally destroyed by their inane gibberish." I went on to explain that though I was not one of the elected co-captains, and rarely first man, they expected me to lead them through the traditional "stare down" at the starting line in order to intimidate the enemy, a Granada Hills ritual that often led to words and scuffles. I begged Godfrey to force the captains to fulfill their duties while allowing me to prepare for my race. Leaning back in my chair, I believed I had stated my case with clarity and articulation.

Coach Godfrey had listened quietly, occasionally nodding his head. This was a three-time state Coach of the Year. When Granada Hills encountered a particularly tough opponent, Godfrey would turn red in the face and roar, "They all wipe their butts the same way." He was a wise old running guru who had been through the battles and won the wars. In the hills, he whipped his teams into shape aboard his Honda 50, which had been a gift from the booster club. During our meets at Pierce College, he would get within inches of our faces at the base of Pukes Peak in order to question our manhood.

Coach Godfrey stared at me for a moment, and then grinned. "Listen to me carefully, Kent," he said. I sensed I had blundered. "Number one: rejoice in the gift that men will gather under your leadership. Few possess such charisma. Despite your reluctance, you exhibit bona fide courage and bravado and the team senses it. Number two: don't ever speak to me in that familiar tone again, you whiney little snot." That got my attention. "This is a two-time defending L.A. City Championship team desperately searching for a leader, and they chose *you*! And all I'm hearing is 'me, myself, and I'. Shame on you. Sometimes responsibility is thrust upon us and a man will rise to the occasion, while a whiney little snot will complain about it to his coach. If you let this team down, I will write to every prospective college that you are a gutless whore who doesn't deserve to be a scholarship athlete. Now get the hell out of my office before I put my foot up your ass."

Needless to say, I got the hell out of his office.

The humiliation stung, but coach was correct. He earned my respect. He shamed and inspired me to become his team leader.

# ONE

## Pop Quiz

*"It is rude to count people as you
pass them, out loud."*

–Adidas

Simple question. Please think carefully before answering.

Given the choice, would a competitive runner prefer: A) win a race or age group with a mediocre or even lousy time, or B) finish in the pack with a personal record?

Please think carefully before answering. The correct answer is on the next page.

Answer: Without a doubt or hesitation, a high school, college, or any other competitive runner should always pick A.

The heart and soul of competitive running is to kick ass, and the more ass kicked the better. Placing well is the ultimate goal. Never fret about times. Times and PR's have little or no meaning to the competitive runner. Kicking ass has meaning. You're only as good as the competition. Times and PR's will come with good competition.

How many Olympians would give up their medal for a PR or even world record? It doesn't make sense. Records are broken, but no one can take away a victory.

For years my personal hero was Roger Bannister, the British runner who was the first to crack the four-minute mile barrier, until I discovered he broke the four-minute mile barrier by using pacers. He even had the 220 splits yelled to him. There was little competition other than the stopwatch. It was an amazing accomplishment, but hardly a competiton.

My new hero became Oregon runner Steve Prefontaine. "Pre" ran against all types of competition and kicked ass. When he kicked good ass, he ran good times. The desire to place well is of paramount importance to the competitive runner, times are merely the results given after a race.

For those who picked B, please do not take offense or put down this book…yet. In fact, if you picked B this book may have more relevance. You probably think I tricked you, which is partially true. A PR against superior competition IS a victory. Sorry, let's let bygones be bygones. But in order for a competitive runner to be successful, a new mindset must be developed. Though no runner wins every race or runs every race well, it must be the mindset of every competitive runner to treat every race as a battle. To battle like a warrior and never settle for less should be every competitive runner's mantra. Run with razors and soul. I define razors as the sharpened edge of physical and mental toughness. And soul is the heart, guts and desire.

If you agree with this philosophy, welcome aboard. Go back and pick A, and prepare to kick ass.

Please do not misunderstand. There is nothing wrong with PR's or placing $2^{nd}$, $5^{th}$, $20^{th}$ or $6,503^{rd}$ in a race. Nothing is wrong with lifting one's butt from the sofa and running to get in shape. But for the competitive runner, there is something inherently pathetic about stepping up to a starting line and thinking, "Boy, I hope I set a PR," oblivious of the ass you are kicking or more importantly the ass that's kicking your ass. When I was a cross country coach, kicking ass became my daily sermon. If someone passes you, take the offensive and latch on. If someone is in front of you, plot to pass.

By no stretch of the imagination was I a great runner. I was okay. Though I beat 85% of the runners I faced, I could have done better, much better. Nothing is more painful than to have that realization when it's too late to make a change. If only I had possessed more guts and determination. If only I hadn't been afraid to attack every race and really uncork a few. If only I hadn't become so easily discouraged and settled for my position in the race, no telling how high I might have soared. Unfortunately, by the time I learned most of what I'll share in this book, I had already retired.

# TWO

## Love

*"Too soon we breast the tape, too late we find the fun lay in the running."*
                                              –Walt Kelly

In the beginning, you must love the sport. Do not bother with track, cross country, or this book if you lack the love. You can't just love to train or race, you must love to run.

Running is pure joy. Running must be in your soul. You must love running for the sake of running. You cannot train and compete to your full potential without the love. Respect your running. Remember: running is the oldest and most natural human sport. Live it, breathe it, sleep it, eat it and enjoy.

Run with razors and soul. Otherwise, do not read this book. Put it down. Get a refund. Running loves you, but it doesn't need you. If you don't love it, your rival will.

During my tenth grade cross country season, Coach Giles Godfrey had the entire tenth grade, junior varsity and varsity run a four-mile time trial. I was injured and stood with Coach Godfrey and our three managers recording times at the finish. Senior Bill King won that time trial by over a minute. When he came into view, he was running fast and smooth with a huge grin on his face. It was his grin that spoke to me. It spoke volumes of his love and respect for the sport. Bill King became my new hero.

In L.A. when it rains, it doesn't quit. It rains long and hard. There is never a quick shower or afternoon sprinkle. When it rains, it's an all-out assault on the entire basin for two to three days, no breaks. For two days the cross country team ran intervals and fartleks under the pavilions on campus. It was boring, hard on the feet and felt like track. On the third day, the varsity decided to take matters in hand and venture into the storm. It began to rain harder. Seven shirtless kids with long hair running along Chatsworth Avenue soaked to the bone was a rare sight in Granada Hills. We endured honks, jeers and girls yelling out their phone numbers. Rain hit us in the face so hard it stung. It was marvelous and we loved it. Running in a small pack and splashing through the puddles helped tighten our bond. On that day we left our love of the sport on those drenched streets.

Never forget that running involves pain, suffering and sacrifice. It is spiritual and religious. It is orgasmic. Don't be a glory hound or race whore. Above all else, love your sport.

# THREE

## Belief

*"Whether you believe you can or believe
you can't, you're probably right."*
—Henry Ford

As simple as the concept sounds, it still must be stated: believe in yourself. Sometimes this is only words and more words. There must be conviction. You must mean it when you say, "I believe in myself." Far too many runners, at the first indication of a struggle, no longer believe. "I'm out of gas, I don't believe I can keep up." This is classic mental breakdown and it happens to every runner at some point.

Unfortunately, most runners don't believe in themselves. Not really. For many runners, belief is fickle and temporary. Since belief in oneself is fleeting, it is crucial to maintain a constant vigil. Day and night, race after race. You must believe in your ability and believe your ability will improve through your training. Training will not only improve your ability, it will also boost your confidence, and confidence will result in belief.

On the morning of the 1966 L.A. City Championships, the Granada Hills Highlander varsity was not favored. Palisades had beaten the team in the prelims, and the newspapers were predicting an end to the dynasty. We were all a little down with resignation. Mike Lampson asked me to gather the seniors under a large eucalyptus tree with a wide-open view of the Valley.

I stood in a circle with Lampson, Paul Burch, Tom Horton, Jim Hanifan, Mike Baker and Alan Silver. Lampson pointed north across the Valley toward Granada Hills. We could clearly see Mission Peak towering above the J. Paul Getty oil fields.

He said, "We've trained our asses off on those hills for three years and today is our last high school race. How do we want to go out?"

"Champions," we said in unison.

"No one expects it. They don't believe we can do it. When we win today, I want all of us to remember this moment for the rest of our lives."

We believed and won by four points.

If there is any doubt concerning your belief, the answer is simple. You must change. It starts with better training, physical and mental. Training and confidence will result in belief.

# FOUR

## Mysticism

*"You just kind of have faith. If that sounds mystical, it's because I don't really know how it works, but I trust that it does."*
    –Richard Russo

No matter what you have heard or believe, there is a higher power. What that means I can't say. But since there is a force, an inner light, a Tao or a band of transcendental electricity running through the air, rocks, trees, water and fiber of every living thing, it certainly cannot be detrimental to the competitive runner to plug into that power. No other explanation should be required.

Concentration, meditation, self-hypnosis or prayer will work. But the intent must be to the glorification of the mind, the body and the indefinable–spirit, soul, or whatever you choose to call it. A runner's soul must be pure and never selfish. From a psychological standpoint, to connect your desire and belief with a divine power can only have positive results.

Without horses until the arrival of the Europeans, running often took on a mystical quality among Native American cultures. Food and survival were at stake. Running was incorporated into religion through vision running and ceremonies.

Among the Apache, it was accepted that warriors who could not keep up while hunting game or escaping enemies would be left behind.

The Running Gods have blessed you with ability and potential. Don't waste it. Rise above your five senses in order to achieve a mystical edge.

# FIVE

## The Importance of a Coach

*"Good coaches show the path,
not the shortcuts."*
                    –Unknown

Good coaches are not rare. They are out there, and they are essential. Never underestimate to contributions of a good coach.

Most important is to have a coach who truly cares and is not just collecting a supplement. The coach does not have to be an ex-champion, track guru or even a former runner. But a good coach must understand the meaning of commitment. All runners need a coach who will guide, listen, massage the fragile ego and deliver the swift kick in the ass when needed. What a runner does not need is the basketball, weightlifting or softball coach taking charge by default and masquerading as a track coach by providing a warm body.

Do not be coached by a book…like this one, for instance. Read it, gather tips, store ideas and then push it aside. This book isn't even a warm body. The coach is there every day.

I was never an individual champion. In cross country, I was a capable top ten runner in high school finals and college invitationals. In track I was nearly always the number one man in my event, which usually translated into first or second place.

But I never won individual championships. My main claim to fame was being a member of a three-time L.A. City Championship cross country team that lost one race in three years. Our reputation was so complete that when I met runners later in college and mentioned Granada Hills, they were instantly respectful and wary. Every single high school cross country race was a grind because I had to run against my teammates. In my senior year, Granada Hills swept (top five) the eventual league runner-up Monroe High School in a dual meet.

Much of Granada Hills' success must be credited to our three-time Coach of the Year, Giles Godfrey. Though I never truly appreciated my coach at the time, I certainly tip my hat to him today, because I finally grew up and realized his genius. Coach Godfrey doted on us like a kindly grandmother, but with a foot always prepared to kick us in the ass. He was our biggest fan, though most of us were too stupid to notice.

Coach Godfrey would use his Honda 50 motorcycle to accompany us into the J. Paul Getty foothills where he would craft excruciating workouts. We delighted in cursing him when he zoomed past kicking up a rooster tail of dust. But I admit it was reassuring to have him with us on those lonely dirt roads and trails. Plus, he was good company. He demonstrated his concern for us every day by being there, rather than sending us out on our own and sitting in an air conditioned office collecting a supplement.

Godfrey's forte was playing us off one another, pulling us aside individually to pump up our confidence. He made each one of us believe we could be the number one man on the team. After Mike Lampson narrowly beat me by one second in a cross country race against Reseda, Godfrey pulled me aside and insisted I was the superior runner and all I needed to do was to dig deeper and believe in myself. Later I caught him telling Lampson he should never allow Kent to be that close and all he needed to do was to stay determined and focused. I was not offended because I knew the score. His well-designed pep talks kept us sharp and competitive. "Don't strut up to the starting line with your press clippings pinned to your shirt," he would bellow. "No one gives a shit what happened last week."

At cross country meets, Coach created a luxurious atmosphere for his teams that made us feel like cross country royalty. There was a camper and tent for race preparation and recuperation. Team managers waited on us, providing liniments, new spikes or shoelaces, and hot tea with honey before each race. Our sweats and uniforms were always of the finest quality. At least fifty people traveled on the team bus, ten runners each on the tenth grade, junior varsity and varsity squads, team managers, assistant coaches and even cheerleaders. Add to that a convoy of parents, friends and girlfriends in private cars and it was an entourage. After holding hands for the traditional prayer, the team would jog to the starting line with a swagger and proceed to stare down the opposing team. It was an unspoken rule that Granada Hills never approached the starting line first. To lose was inconceivable. We had the runners, we completed the workouts and we had the coach.

Team protocol dictated that the junior varsity and varsity accompanied the tenth grade team to the starting line and collected their sweats and warm-up shoes. After the tenth graders finished their race, the varsity would lend a shoulder to each runner for the trip back to the tent for water, oxygen and to collect their finish tickets. As a tenth grader, having my varsity hero Bill King help me with my sweats after a race meant the world. The tenth grade would do the same for the junior varsity and the junior varsity helped the varsity. A Granada Hills meet was an event. Coach Godfrey made us feel special and his teams won ten of twelve championships in four years.

Pat Connolly was a former UCLA track star and founder of the Encino Track Club. On weekends, Connolly coached dozens of the best runners in the Valley, regardless of their school affiliation. He could talk to twenty runners during a tough workout and make it feel like he was talking only to you.

Connolly preached relaxation, especially during races, and mental toughness. He stressed establishing the perfect game plan for each race, and then bolstered your desire and confidence. My best tips for race-day preparation were learned from Pat Connolly.

Kurt Nelson was the cross country and track coach at California Lutheran University in Thousand Oaks. Though a science professor and weightlifting coach with virtually no running experience, Coach Nelson possessed an amazing gift to say the perfect thing at the right time. He was uncanny. There wasn't an ounce of flattery or bullshit in his huge frame. If you sucked, he'd tell you so in colorful terms. But during a race, if he said you could win, though you had already quit because the two leaders were kicking dirt in your face, you believed him. He could spot a weakness and assess the entire breakdown of a race in a few seconds. The CLU runners were grateful to have him in our corner.

Also, for a guy with no running experience, Coach Nelson put together the finest cross-training workouts on the planet.

# SIX

## Stress

*"The will to win means nothing if you haven't the will to prepare."*
—Juma Ikangaa

Competitive running can be quite stressful. The pressure to perform is intense. It's also an ego thing. Your worth as an individual is being tested. Big races can be unnerving because there's no place to hide on the starting line.

To combat stress, pressure and mental hype, my number one weapon was to put in the training. The knowledge that you have logged the hours, days and weeks with speed, intervals and distance will provide an immense psychological boost before an important race. My worst nightmare was to be standing on the starting line knowing I had not put in the proper training.

Weapon number two is the relaxation techniques taught by Coach Pat Connolly of UCLA, which will be discussed in a later chapter. Stay in the shade and do not exert yourself until warm-ups. Leave the chatter on the bus or in the locker room, inane conversations near the field of battle tend to break your focus and concentration. Pray or meditate. Never, I repeat, never converse with the enemy before a race. There will be plenty of time for chatter and camaraderie after the race. Take a good dump.

Number three is desire. How badly do you want it? Get determined and feed on the stress. Nervous energy before a race is expected and normal. In fact, it's essential. If you can't get emotionally charged before a race, your commitment to the job must be questioned. Sometimes I would be so jacked up with nervous energy before a race, I felt like a thoroughbred horse at the starting gate, stomping and snorting. Use nervous energy as an ally. Welcome those adrenalin shakes and twitches because as soon as the gun sounds that nervous energy will carry you through the first quarter mile before you even think about taking a deep breath. Why is it nearly impossible to duplicate race times during a workout? One reason is that the nervous energy occurs only before a race.

Number four is courage, courage to enter the race in order to pursue your goals. Fear often enters the picture with extreme prejudice. Be courageous and never back down. Number five is to bathe in the encouragement of your coach, teammates, friends, parents, siblings and girlfriends. They will be the nucleus of your support system and help you redirect stress into energy. Number six is to believe. You've done the training. There's no reason why you can't keep up with the pack.

There will be times when none of this will work. Remember: you are human, not a robot. Experience is part of the learning process. Since there will be other races, do not dwell on the past. I retract that statement…use setbacks as motivation for the next race. Defeat can be a powerful ally.

# SEVEN

## *Gender Bias*

*"See Dick run, see Jane run faster."*
–Unknown

I'm a guy. Since I'm a guy, I've only experienced the competitive spirit from a guy's perspective. But I suspect the perspective is universal. Some may assume I'm writing only for guys, and girls are not part of the equation. Not true. I apologize for my gender bias, but I'm still a guy. The qualities and attributes promoted by this book are by no means exclusive to guys. Mary Decker, Joan Benoit, Serena Williams, Gail Devers, Mia Hamm and Lindsey Vonn demonstrate my point. These women had the qualities to win in the face of pain and adversity that I would have given my left testicle (sorry again, girls) to possess. There are countless examples of female athletic excellence. I've seen high school girls raise their performance and refuse to succumb to the fatigue and doubts that sometimes got the best of me.

Hope this clears the air of any gender misconceptions. I'm a guy with male quirks and perspectives, but I'm writing for the runner, no matter the gender, and I promise never, never to say in a derisive manner, "Man, he runs like a girl."

# EIGHT

## Definition of Winning

*"Are you going to be a wimp or are you going to be strong today?"*
            –Peter Maher

I have made it a point to talk about winning and kicking ass. But what is the definition of winning? What is kicking ass?

Is winning placing first? Yep. Top ten? Sure. Top ten in an age group? Of course. Winning is to make an honest and determined effort to attain you goal. Start by putting in an honest effort at training, no shortcuts. Take care of yourself. Make a serious attempt at psychological preparation and commit yourself to good food, sleep and not participating in too many late night activities.

Winning is to eliminate excuses and take a chance at improving your performance. Winning is to eliminate the word "quit" from your vocabulary. It is far too easy to be satisfied with a decent finish rather than question whether or not you ran your best race. It's too easy to settle for your position in a race and not try to move up. After many races, I was cheered and congratulated when in reality I knew in my soul I had settled for a place. Don't be a coward. Dare to take a risk and get better. Dare to discover and nurture your capabilities.

If you can achieve your goals in training, commitment, sacrifice, desire and all the other little things that will add up, and dare to venture out and do your best, then you are a winner. If I've implied anything to the contrary, it was not my intention and I apologize.

I do not hold the typical recreational runner in contempt. However, most recreational runners do not really compete. If you are only concerned with a finish or PR or the thrill of being among 10,000 other runners, you are not really competing. Competitive racing is stressful, explosive, combative, euphoric and sometimes devastating. Running a college two-mile race with ten to fifteen runners whose PR's are within six seconds will test your mettle. The pressure to place well for team, coach, scholarship and ego is intense. Add to the mix that a top four finish means a continuation of the season, and your parents, friends, girlfriend and minister are in attendance...well, that defines "competitive" racing.

# NINE

## Quitting

*"Most people run a race to see who is fastest. I run a race to see who has the most guts."*
—Steve Prefontaine

The majority of runners will swear they never quit during a race. Don't be deceived: they lie. All runners have quit in races. I admit to quitting in a majority of my races. Let me clarify. Most of the time quitting will not be recognized. Quitting can be broken down into three classifications.

Quitting, Class # 1
It is true that few runners make a habit of quitting, class # 1, which is physically stopping during a race and not finishing. Quitting, class # 1 is the ultimate defeat and rarely happens. But it is always out there lurking. I quit class # 1 twice during my career and regret both times. A competitive runner is a failure if he makes quitting, class # 1 habitual.

Quitting, Class # 2
This may be more recognizable. It's a mental quit. Though the body continues to run and

finish the race, the runner has long before quit competing. All the runner desires is to get off the course or track and end the anguish. He is way beyond caring if other runners pass him. Quitting, class # 2 does not automatically translate into a bad race. Usually quitting, class # 2 occurs during the second half of a race, which could mean the majority of the race went well. Some runners PR during quitting, class # 2. But it still qualifies as a quit. Quitting, class # 2 can be a frequent tormentor for good runners, though for recreational runners it could have little or no consequence and may not even be noticed. Finishing a 10K or marathon is a great victory for a recreational runner, even if they did quit class # 2. But to a competitive runner, quitting, class # 2 could be the reason that a major goal was not attained.

Quitting, Class # 3

Class # 3 is subtle and the most dangerous of the quits to a competitive runner. It occurs in most races. Quitting, class # 3 is quitting during a race because you are satisfied with your position. "This is great, I'm in fourth place." I call this "settling." You will settle for a place and finish the race. In fact, you may finish strong and disguise your quitting, class # 3 with a tenacious performance, holding off several rivals for that fourth place. Everyone will slap you on the back and tell you what a great race you ran, and you will feel pretty satisfied about yourself with a trophy or medal in your hand. Some of my best races were run after falling victim to quitting, class # 3. Dangerous and more dangerous. Why? Because you still quit. Quitting, class # 3 means you failed to make the attempt, failed to take a chance, failed to seize the opportunity and failed to rise to the occasion. You succumbed to the intoxication of a good race and sacrificed the possibility of a great race.

This is hard to admit: I won many races with luck and a quitting attitude. One particular invitational serves as an excellent example. During my warm-ups I was determined and fired up. I was in a "kick ass and take no prisoners" mentality. Then I got into the race and worked hard to stay near the front. Deep into the race, however, my tough facade began to crumble. The more it hurt, the more I lost my punch. The more I lost my punch, the more I settled for my place. Running hard is supposed to hurt. Never be surprised by the pain or how bad it hurts. Expect to deal with the hurt in every race. The hurt forced me to abandon my pre-race exuberance. I began to talk myself out of the race. I was quitting. I became a coward and just wanted to finish. My mind was no longer convinced I could keep up, and my body was listening. Sixth place was a very respectable position.

Somehow my conditioning kept me in the race, though my mind had tossed in the towel. My months of strenuous workouts would not allow me to slow down just yet. I was still near the front, but it seemed inevitable that I would lose ground. Suddenly two or three guys fell off the pace. I had outlasted them. The leaders started to come back to me and were obviously struggling. My mind shed off the numbness and realized something important was happening–everyone else was dying too. Then Coach Kurt Nelson pointed a finger and told me I could win. I regained hope. We hit a dip and shot up a short hill, and without even trying I took the lead. No one challenged my move. For the first time in the race, I really believed I could win.

After finishing in first place, I was congratulated ad nauseam. It had been a brilliant race. If only everyone knew how close I had come to quitting. It was a win with luck and a quitting attitude.

# TEN

## Fear

*"Run like you're being chased by a grizzly bear."*
                              –Pat Dooley

For teenagers, Halloween is a night created for mischief. During a 1965 Halloween encounter, involving a barrage of egg throwing, a small group of Granada Hills runners was pursued by a mob of juvenile delinquents. There was certainly no doubt which group would receive the worse end in a confrontation. Jim Evans and I ran so hard we not only escaped, we roared past the defending league 880 champion, and we were two-milers.

The moral of this story is to use fear as an ally. Run like you stole something. Some of my best races resulted from fear. Not from a fear that the runners chasing me would beat my ass if they caught me, but from the fear of embarrassment, insult and humiliation. The fear of getting my ass handed to me was an excellent motivator.

Sometimes before a race I was absolutely terrified I would not perform well. The fear would be paralyzing. Coach Pat Connolly of the Encino Track Club sat me down and said, "There is nothing wrong with your fear. Fear is good. Fear keeps you alive. Fear is the reason the gazelle runs so fast from the lion. What you need to do is transform your fear of a bad performance into adrenaline energy. What's the worst that can happen if you have a bad day? You're not going to die. The gazelle is fearful because if he loses he dies. You, on the other hand, will have countless opportunities to improve. Transform your fear into adrenaline energy and use that energy as an ally. Once the gun goes off, that energy will give you an incredible boost. That is the power of fear."

Fear of failure or humiliation can become one of your best allies. It's amazing how fear can lift desire and determination.

# ELEVEN

## Cross Training

*"Somewhere in the world someone is training when you are not. When you race him he will win."*

−Tom Fleming

Cross training simply means supplemental training. You need to adopt an individual training method, other than running, in order to improve your running. Boxers jump rope, football and basketball players run wind sprints and wrestlers lift weights. There is a wide array of aerobic and strength activities that can improve your performance.

Mike Baker was a friend, teammate and rival during my junior year on the 1965 Granada Hills championship team. Though we appeared equal in ability, I possessed the talent, form, speed and cockiness. He had the guts. He also had a secret weapon.

Following an especially brutal workout that included a tough two-mile time trial on a Himalayan course, where my superior speed had burned Baker on the final flat, I hopped aboard my Honda 250 Scrambler and roared down Chatsworth Avenue hoping to impress the ladies. Mike Baker was walking home, head down and obviously exhausted.

When I pulled over to offer him a ride, he gruffly declined. I always believed it was because I had smoked him in the time trial.

A few months later, after finishing behind Mike Baker twelve out of fourteen races during the season, he asked me for a ride home. As we headed down Chatsworth Avenue on my Honda 250 Scrambler, I asked him why he hadn't accepted my earlier offer. He claimed the brisk four-mile walk home gave him an edge in the meets. He had walked four miles home every day after workouts while I rode my motorcycle trying to impress girls. Mike Baker made sense. I realized the moral to this story was cross training. Adding a new component to the training schedule allowed Baker to achieve a physical as well as mental edge. In order to achieve an advantage, some sort of cross training is necessary. I'm not advocating an additional two-hour grind, just twenty to thirty minutes a day in some other form of activity.

After a banner 1969 track season, I am convinced it was due to my thirty minutes of bicycle riding three days a week. On two other days I swam laps and lifted weights for arm strength. I tricked myself into thinking the bike and swimming regimen was fun. I enjoyed pedaling through my neighborhood checking out the action and girls. The swimming presented an incredible time for reflection with only the sound of my splashing and breathing. It was serene. The cross training increased my aerobic capacity and endurance, and strengthened my arms. Mike Baker had taught me an important lesson.

Don't care for biking or swimming? Try jumping rope, hiking, dancing or an elliptical. Tennis or karate is good. Weights, however, are a must. Don't exclude the weights. By becoming a stronger all-around athlete, you will become a stronger runner.

# TWELVE

## Weights and Alternatives

*"Running is the greatest metaphor for life, because you get out of it what you put into it."*
                                    –Oprah Winfrey

Weight training definitely has its place in the routine of a competitive runner. Three times a week for twenty minutes. Nothing heavy. It's all about upper body strength. Never work the legs with weights. Allow only your running to work the legs. Knee bends, squats and leg weights only tend to strain and pull muscles, ligaments and tendons. Don't do it! The weights are for the arms and shoulders, which can be an incredible asset when the arms and shoulders feel like logs near the end of a race.

Early in my career, I noticed arm and shoulder weakness long before leg fatigue. Hills in cross country or gun laps in track can really take a toll on the upper body. The legendary "bear" delights in jumping on your back at the end of a race. Weights will help you slide the bear off your back.

Curls and military and bench presses should do the trick. I recommend three reps of fifteen for each exercise, using forty to ninety pounds. Take a five or ten-pound dumbbell in each hand and pump your arms as if you are running for five minutes. Once again, the weights should be light. There is no need to be buff. The benefits of weights are your strength and tone.

To survive long distances, all runners need upper body strength, especially in the shoulders. If you don't favor the bulk or tightness that may accompany weight training, try lighter weights. If that still causes discomfort, here are some alternatives.

Try pull-ups and push-ups. These exercises are more natural and usually don't cause the stiffness and bulk of weights.

Swimming is an excellent activity. Swim short sprints at top speed. This will increase endurance and improve arm strength. Try water running. Place your entire body in about five feet of water and run around a small area of the pool, pumping your arms. Ten to twenty minutes should leave you panting.

My favorite alternative to weight training was to punch the heavy bag. This can be a surprisingly effective workout and will immediately improve arm and shoulder strength. After fifteen to twenty minutes, you will gain an immense respect for boxers.

# THIRTEEN

## Seasons

*Everybody can't be good, there has to be somebody to stand on the curb and cheer us on."*
—Bill Rodgers

No runner can stay in peak condition year round. In fact, no runner should even attempt to keep up a rigid training schedule year round. There will be highs, lows and plateaus. Add the fatigue and burnout factor, and it becomes necessary for a runner to design his training for the seasons. For the high school and college runner there is no confusion—cross country and track (indoor and outdoor) seasons. For the competitive roadrunner, you must choose the important races and design your season so that you peak for those races.

Since the fatigue factor is an inevitable component, you must plan your non-seasons for rest and relaxation. Rest between the cross country and track seasons, and again between track in the spring and cross country in the fall. This does not mean to stop running. It means to slack off. I'm a huge advocate of year round training, a must for the successful runner. Some of my most oppressive weeks of existence were the boring summer workouts. But training between the seasons should be light, loose, relaxing and fun. Rejuvenation is the key word. A tough season can be draining. During your off-season you only need to maintain a relaxed running condition, so when the intensity of a new season is about to begin you are rested but not out of shape.

Workouts between the seasons should include cross training and long, relaxing runs that include loads of conversation and laughter with friends and teammates. Mike Lampson, Richard Knapp and I loved to combine surfing safaris with running safaris. After a pleasant morning of surfing, a slow run on the beach with buddies was a pleasure.

Our favorite beach to run after a morning of surfing was Point Dume cove just south of Zuma Beach. The beach had nicely packed sand and high cliffs that discouraged the family and beach bunny crowd. We liked to run about four miles to the end of the point, and sit on the rocks to watch the swells before running back. It would have been nice to run around the point, but the tide was always too high. One day the sand was visible and a run seemed manageable. We decided to seize the day. Running into the second cove, we nearly blundered into the space of over fifty people lounging on the legendary Nude Beach. "I didn't think it existed," Lampson said. We immediately reversed our direction and picked up the pace.

# FOURTEEN

## Obvious Department

*"Cross country is the reason I drink...
lots of water."*
−Unknown

Common sense dictates another essential component to successful competitive running: take care of yourself.

Take care of yourself with tons of sleep, proper nutrition and vitamins, loading up on the C, E and B family. Do not smoke, marijuana included. Do not drink alcohol, although moderate amounts of beer or wine are okay for the twenty-one and over gang. Take extreme precautions against illness, and initiate fanatical care when illness strikes. It is discouraging what the flu or serious respiratory infection can do to the middle of a season. Baby yourself.

Legendary University of Oregon coach Bill Bowerman was a zealot when it came to foot care. He espoused proper socks, liniments and shoes in order to protect the foot from strains, blisters, bone bruises and heel spurs. Foot massages became a major activity among his runners. His obsession with footwear (he developed a shoe with a special bottom pad on a waffle iron) led to him co-founding Nike.

# FIFTEEN

## Buddy Running

*"True friendship comes when the silence
between people is comfortable."*
–David Tyson Gentry

The more buddies the merrier. But it is
critical that you find at least one good buddy for a
training partner. Your buddy should be available for
after-hours psychological support. It is ideal to pick
someone who is slightly faster than you, but if
everyone followed that advice no one would have a
buddy.

I was lucky. In my junior year I picked
Richard Knapp. Richard wasn't even on the varsity;
he was a member of the junior varsity. I could beat
him handily in a three mile cross country race, but
in workouts over four miles Richard began to click.
One afternoon I watched him run away from Keith
Cooney on a ten-mile run, and Cooney was the
varsity league champ.

Chasing or holding off a runner of equal
talent is mutually beneficial to both runners.
Richard and I were not equals. On short surges or
intervals he chased me. Beyond four miles I
couldn't beat him. Training with Richard in the
distances was an incredible boost to my endurance
and confidence. If I could hang with Richard for

eight miles, I could hang with nearly anyone for that distance.

Workouts have the potential to be intense and dynamic. The faster buddy will attempt to establish dominance while the slower buddy will work like a dog to not let it happen. Buddies keep each other sharp. During my entire eleventh grade varsity season, I trained with Richard Knapp, who never beat me in a three-mile race. However, I never beat him in a workout over four miles and neither did anyone else on the varsity. We ran some spectacular distance workouts. When Richard finished third in the junior varsity City finals and I broke into the top four on our varsity City Championship team, it was a victory for our training partnership.

Buddies are crucial during the two-a-day workout portion of the season (see chapter seventeen). They are crucial in getting you up early in the morning and keeping you out late in the afternoon. Buddies can also help you push through the cross training burdens of weights, swimming or bicycling.

Also, communication was a key to our workouts because it kept us connected. I did most of the communicating for the first four miles and Richard Knapp did all the communicating thereafter. We talked and joked, insulted and laughed, in order to encourage and relax. More importantly, we talked to remain in contact. This strategy easily carried over into races. I enjoyed having conversations while competing.

# SIXTEEN

## Teammates

*"Really get to know your teammates because they are your new family and they will be the ones there for you when anything goes wrong."*
—Alex Morgan

Teammates. It's a simple word that has decisive meaning. Granada Hills High School developed a list of traditions among teammates, regardless of individual success, competition or personal hatred. Those traditions included warming up with each other before every race, collecting the sweats and warm-up shoes from the tenth grade and junior varsity before their races, carrying the tenth graders and junior varsity back to the camper for tea and water after their races, jogging together to the starting line, staring down the opponents as we took up our positions on the line, huddling in a circle to hold hands for a prayer, shouting "GH" at the gun, maintaining contact and communication during the race, and confronting opponents after the race, if necessary.

Teammates must get along. There's nothing wrong with arguments or wanting to kick each other's ass. But during the season you are on the same team and you stick by each other, period. You are family. You don't have to like everyone or even be friends, but during the season teammates must be brothers-in-arms.

I wanted terribly to beat every one of my teammates in every single race, and they likewise wanted to beat me. We were not secret about it either. The desire and obsession to beat each other made us tough. Remember: I had to run against these guys in every workout and every race. No one is at the top of his or her game for every workout or every race, but at least one of your teammates will be feeling his oats during every workout and every race, and that teammate will be the instigator.

It is unbelievable what a tight group of teammates can accomplish together. Reseda High School finished third in the 1966 L.A. City finals and had two top ten City finishers. But on the day Reseda High School ran a dual meet with Granada Hills, the defending city champions, there was nowhere to hide and every runner was in plain view. Running on a downhill curve, our top six surrounded their big two and proceeded to bump, jostle, talk and do whatever was necessary to rattle, intimidate or at least piss off the two enemy runners in order to gain an edge. It also kept our six together; no one dared to drift back. I would have rather faced a firing squad than fallen back and had to face my teammates after the race. The Reseda boys battled gallantly, but they were clearly overmatched psychologically and appeared to sense it. It was a Granada Hills day, the Reseda big two finished fifth and seventh. Though the seventh place runner beat us all in the finals, we never saw him during the race. If the City meet had been held with only Granada Hills and Reseda, the results might have been the same as the dual meet. Granada Hills knew how to intimidate.

Obviously, training together was the key. I ran some of the finest and most glorious races of my career on the J. Paul Getty oil fields north of Granada Hills, with no spectators, officials, timers, trophies or press. Ordinary workouts would transform into blood feuds. To win one of those races could be the grandest moment of the season. Why? Because they were my teammates, and you should always have more respect for your teammates than for any other runner.

# SEVENTEEN

## Two-a-Days

*"Some people train knowing they're not working as hard as other people. I can't fathom how they think."*
—Alberto Salazar

Two-a-days are paramount for a successful season, but only at the proper time. For one thing, a runner should never do two-a-days in the early weeks of the season in order to catch up or get in shape quickly. This will only increase your chances for soreness and injury. Soreness and injury at the beginning of the season can be major setbacks and have negative effects on your mental energy. This isn't football. A runner must be in pretty good shape to tackle two-a-days. But at the proper time in a season, two-a-days can help a runner break out of a rut or plateau and push to the next level.

Since the seasons of cross country and track usually build to a county, league, district, regional, etc., achieving peak condition at the most important part of the season is critical. Runners can usually hold peak condition for three to four races. After that you may plateau or even decline slightly. The most common mistake of a competitive runner is to peak too soon. League champions failing to qualify at the next level may not be the norm, but it happens. Two-a-days must be carefully planned in order to achieve peak condition at the optimal point in the season.

It is recommended two-a-days be initiated for a maximum of three weeks some time before the first important qualifying race. It's up to the individual runner to choose which qualifying race is most important, keeping in mind that non-qualifiers will have ended their seasons.

Quick review: three weeks maximum with the two-a-day regimen per season. Maintain a serious vigil for the fatigue factor and taper off if it becomes a struggle. Stop one week before your first major qualifying race. During two-a-days do not neglect your nutrition or sleep. Time must be sacrificed for the body to recover, heal and refresh. After you finish your two-a-days, mini two-a-days (no more than twice a week) can maintain or even elevate your condition.

A standard two-a-day schedule mixes distance runs with intervals. Usually the morning session is reserved for the long runs and the afternoon for the serious work. My Granada Hills teammates and I developed a slightly different agenda. We liked to do the distance work at night. Running on a hilly golf course at night, with the sprinklers and cool mist in the air, is still in my blood. I can still taste the smell of wet grass and eucalyptus.

A typical two-a-day consisted of six to eight miles of afternoon interval work. Any combination of running a mile, 1320 or 880 at a hard pace, followed by a very easy 440 for recovery, and then on to another hard interval. Continue. I try not to mention times because a five-minute split might be too fast for some or too slow for others. You make the adjustments. The evening run should be five to eight miles at medium pace.

# EIGHTEEN

## Off Days

*"This sport would be cool if it wasn't
for all the running."*
                                              –Unknown

Off days are indispensable for recuperation. The body and mind require a break, even for the high school and college runner. Six out of seven days a week for training is sufficient.

The weekly grind and stress of workouts and races will take a toll. Reward yourself once a week with a day off. Your day off should include a luxurious hot bath, nine to ten hours sleep and a relaxing evening parked on a couch in front of the TV. The off days each week will soothe sore calves and ankles, ease tender groin and hamstring muscles, and heal the strained back, knees and hip. If you race once a week, I recommend the day before or after the race. It's your call. Rest will rejuvenate the legs and provide a psychological boost. I'm serious. Far too many runners suffer from burnout in the middle of a season. Off days should be your reward for putting in the hours. Once added to the routine, I guarantee you will work harder and look forward to your off day.

# NINETEEN

## Five-Quick-Steps

*"To give anything less than your best
is to give away the gift."*
—Steve Prefontaine

One of the most important tricks to learn for a successful competitive runner is the five-quick-steps technique. As you are running, lean forward, shorten your stride, lift your knees and pump your arms. Hit five quick shortened steps for an increase in speed. Think of it as shifting gears.

My favorite spot on the track to use the five-quick-steps was coming out of the curves onto the straights. At the top of the curve, begin to lean forward in preparation and pull your arms in closer to your chest. When you hit the straight, employ the five-quick-steps for a short surge down the track. The next trick is to use the five-quick-steps, and then be able to recover from the effort. You may want to try it again later in the race.

Five-quick-steps is essential for passing or holding off another runner. If you inch past an opponent, nine out of ten times he will speed up and keep pace with you. Take them by surprise and with authority. You will inflict a psychological wound. Five-quick-steps will give you the jump and take the fight out of them, especially if you not only get past but pull a few yards ahead.

In cross country or road races, five-quick-steps will help you regain the pace after going around a post, or sharp turn, or reaching the top of a difficult hill. Here is where you must dare to attack. Hit the top of the hill or go around that cone with five-quick-steps and take the initiative. In the final sprint, five-quick-steps will help you reach your maximum speed quickly and gain the momentum to the chute or finish line. The advanced runner will use the five-quick-steps to pull away from a stubborn rival, and then return to the pace. If a rival is approaching, nothing can dampen their spirit or confidence more than the five-quick-steps.

Train for the five-quick-steps every day. Work and concentrate on recovery. Run 220's with the first 110 medium speed, five-quick-steps, and the second 110 medium-hard. Run 440's with the first 220 medium speed, five-quick-steps, and the second 220 medium-hard. Run 880's with the first 440 medium speed, five-quick-steps, and the second 440 medium-hard. You get the idea. Run miles medium-easy with five-quick-steps coming out of every curve for twenty yards, and then recover the pace until the next curve. Practice running hills at medium speed, with five-quick-steps at the top for a twenty yard surge.

One of the most common ways to practice the five-quick-steps is to get seven guys to run single file at a medium-easy pace. Every fifteen to twenty seconds, have the last runner take five-quick-steps and surge into the lead. Once he settles back down to the pace, the last runner will count to twenty before he does the five-quick-steps and takes the lead. Continue for two to four miles.

During a two-mile race at Fremont High School, two runners from Fremont tried to pass Chuck Franklin and me three times in the final two laps. On each attempt, Chuck or I tapped the other on the elbow and nodded, and then we applied the five-quick-steps. After each surge, we eased back into our pace and concentrated on recovery, which I believe is physically more difficult than the steps, which are actually more mental. I listened intently for the clicking of their spikes on the last curve for a final attempt, but they had apparently settled for third and fourth.

Five-quick-steps is a training strategy that can expand your racing tactics, boost psychological conditioning and sharpen quickness. It can take you to the next level.

# TWENTY

## The Importance of a Kick

*Running takes balls, other sports just play with them."*

–Unknown

No one is expected to be a Carl Lewis or Usain Bolt, but a dependable kick is not to be overlooked. Training to develop a kick is crucial. Some have it naturally and are just plain swift, but the majority of distance runners must develop a kick by selling their soul to the devil or through plain hard work.

I'm not speaking necessarily of a blinding final hundred-yard sprint. My final one hundred yards was mediocre at best. The kick I'm referring to is a sustaining drive with a 330, 440 or 550 to go that aims to win the battle by attrition. Its goal is to punish the opponent mentally and drag out of him any final burst of speed. Frank Shorter summed it up by saying, "I destroyed him."

With hard work and resolve, you can gain confidence in your kick and learn to depend on it. You will gain a reputation that will be as meaningful as the kick itself. Other runners will become wary and you will have a mental edge, especially if they can't shake you during the race.

In a cross country race at California State Fullerton, I hung with the lead group of enemy runners until the final hill, and then broke away to win. During the track season those same runners remembered. In the two-mile, I ran on the shoulder of their big man and hung on for dear life. To my amazement, on the seventh lap his entire distance team lined the back straightaway and shouted, "He's still there, Henry," "Henry, that's not enough," and "You gotta lose him, Henry." I was in pain and very near settling for second place, but their words of warning to Henry aroused me. I realized that Henry remembered our cross country race and was intimidated by my kick. Game on. When I rallied and began my surge at the 550 mark, Henry rolled over. As I said, I was never a particularly fast fifty to one hundred yard sprinter, but I did develop a strong 440-550 surge in the two and three-mile that was a weapon. Naturally, it was all about training.

During workouts, run 880, 1320 and mile intervals with a final surge in mind. Run the interval at medium speed, with the final lap at medium-hard. Work the five-quick-steps in order to shift gears. Most importantly, when the final 550-440 arrives in the race, dare to initiate the surge and don't hold back.

The golden rule for speed work is grass only. The next rule for speed work is grass as much as possible. I realize it's difficult, but speed work should always be done on grass or soft dirt. The hard pounding on pavement or cinder is hell on ankles, shins and knees. Use the grass between the goal posts on the track, or the inside of the track, or parks, golf courses, soccer fields, or the medians of boulevards. Use dirt roads. For a real treat, try the soft sand at the beach.

Pavement is just no good on the body. The continual pounding on pavement will deaden your natural spring and expose you to a plethora of potential injuries. Distance running on pavement may be tolerable, but it is not recommended. There is no excuse for sprinting on pavement. Maybe the young can survive, but I said maybe. Many young runners don't make it through a season or to college because of pavement related injuries. On rainy days in high school I ran on pavement in order to utilize the covered walkways. Running on streets in college I began to experience injuries. After Coach Pat Connolly coaxed me back onto the grass and dirt the injuries vanished.

Another excellent reason to train on grass is the grand transformation you will experience on a track or paved course after training on the mush. Traction and bounce are magnified. You will feel fast and strong, and you will be fast and strong.

# TWENTY-ONE

## Plan Your Kick

*"Today I will run what you will not, so
that tomorrow I will run what you cannot."*
                                        –Unknown

Planning your kick must include the mantra: "Never hold back in order to preserve a kick." Does that make sense? Okay, it's silly to save energy for a kick because there are far better strategies, and if you wait until the kick to make your move it may be too late. Planning is the key.

Don't hesitate when you think it is time to initiate a kick. Hesitation is often the difference between winning and losing. Many times, whoever gets off first and establishes momentum will take the place. Don't be afraid to be first. Don't be afraid to carry out a plan. Don't hesitate.

At times it may be wise to observe the moves of an opponent and to react to those moves with strategy. If you possess blazing speed, much of this chapter need not apply. If your kick is only good or average, getting the jump, hitting the five-quick-steps and maintaining a relaxed stride are the strategies that must be practiced during your training in order to develop a kick that becomes a weapon.

As stated earlier, my weakness was the final one hundred yards. I didn't die or slow down, I just lacked the acceleration and speed to overtake or hold off the good ones. My advantage was that I knew it. I compensated by developing a 550-440 kick. If an opponent couldn't keep up, his kick would be of no use at the end of the race. If he was still there, hopefully my surge had weakened his kick. If I still got beat, at least I went down swinging on my own terms.

None of my lessons came easy. In fact, all of them were acquired through pain and suffering which translated into experience. Many of the lessons had to be learned more than once. I was never a quick study. Intelligent running is not inherent; it is an acquired talent. Many of the best lessons are learned under extreme conditions that may turn ugly. The trick is to turn the adversity, disastrous decisions and humiliating races into lessons that will improve and enlighten you. The experience will transform into wisdom.

In a cross country race against Chapman University on their home course, I dogged their two best runners for most of the race. With a glance, they signaled each other and got the jump on me. I managed to stay on their heels to the chute, but the damage had been done. I might have beaten one or both had I gotten off first. Maybe not, but I'll never know since I allowed them to make the first move on their home course. In fact, I was unfamiliar with the course and had no idea where the chute was located. Another lesson: know the course and don't run blind. Walk or jog as much of the course as possible before the race. If possible, run the course in advance, then position a manager or friend near the spot you plan to start your kick.

# TWENTY-TWO

## Sing a Song

*"Racing teaches us to challenge ourselves.*
*It helps us to find out what we are made of."*
                                        —PattiSue Plumer

For workouts, and especially during races, choose a favorite song that will stimulate and keep you chugging. It might even take your mind off the pain. Hum or sing the song in your head while running. Think of it as a form of self-hypnosis. It may help you get over the hump or through the wall. Practice the tactic during workouts.

Never tell a soul your secret song. If you do, the power of the song will be lost. Mike Lampson taught me this trick in tenth grade. It was a fascinating idea, but when I inquired about his song he went mum. Never share your song, he warned. To this day he has not told me. I can tell you mine: *All Day and All of the Night* by the Kinks.

# TWENTY-THREE

## Visuals

*"I've had as many doubts as anyone else.
Standing on the starting line, we're all
cowards."*
                                        −Alberto Salazar

Much ballyhoo has been made about
visualizing a race before it happens. As you
visualize, you plan strategy, surges and victory. It's
a cool idea, but total nonsense. This strategy may
work in golf, diving or field events in track, but not
distance running. Distance running has too many
unforeseen circumstances, including weather,
challenging courses and the opposition. There are
far too many variables in a distance race for it to
unfold the way you visualized. You must prepare
for the unexpected and be spontaneous. If you
visualize a race in a certain way, and for whatever
reason the race deviates from that vision, the
psychological damage may be irreversible.

A different form of visualization may be
more appropriate. Visualize your favorite place in
the world. Mine was Point Dume near Zuma Beach.
Use this visual, much like your song, as a sort of
mesmerization in order to get over the hump or
through the wall. Visualize your favorite place, sing
your song, and hang onto it like grim death until

you are ready to make your move. This form of visualization makes sense and may override the pain of the race. As usual, if you can master this form of visualization in practice it will become second nature during a race. All tricks work better if they have been fine-tuned during training.

# TWENTY-FOUR

## Hot Baths

*"There must be quite a few things that
a hot bath won't cure, but I don't know
many of them."*
                                        —Sylvia Plath

You need hot baths five to seven nights a week for twenty minutes, if possible. The night before a race is an absolute. Nothing soothes the legs after a tough workout better than a hot bath. If you live in luxury, Jacuzzis or hot tubs will suffice. I've always preferred a hot bath, however, because as the temperature decreases you will know when it is time to get out.

There is a procedure to be obeyed: 1) Hot as you can take it; 2) Submerge slowly—feet, shins, butt, thigh—and then sit in the tub in order to stretch out the legs; 3) Never lower the upper body into the water until the end of the soak. You don't run with your chest.

Hot baths should be an integral part of your leg maintenance. It might get a little sweaty in there, though. You may want to position a fan or open a window. Also, have a tall glass of water within reach.

After your bath, go directly to bed. Once in bed, you will feel a refreshing tingle. The hot bath will put the spring back into your legs.

# TWENTY-FIVE

## Sleep

*"Spend at least some of your training time, and other parts of the day, concentrating on what you are doing in training and visualize your success."*

–Greta Waitz

I am a huge fan of sleep. Do not allow the armies of fatigue to amass their troops on your border. Runners cannot reach their potential without being well rested. Following a difficult workout, sleep is necessary for the body to recover physically and mentally. Loads of sleep can also ward off illness.

Sleep must be consistent. A fourteen-hour night of sleep in order to make up for the four hours the night before is fine once in a while, but should not be habitual. Sleep is accumulated. It must be part of the regimen and planned in advance. You must sacrifice to make it happen. Unfortunately, that means fewer wild and crazy nights during the season. Keep a journal of your sleep hours. In fact, now might be a good time to mention a running journal to chart your workouts. You can enter data into both journals at bedtime. You need your sleep in order to maintain a rugged training schedule. Race preparation demands clarity, alertness and desire. A fatigued runner will lack the zip needed to perform and concentrate.

Naps can work. Though not as effective as an uninterrupted night of sleep, a nap can be rejuvenating and offer a sound alternative.

A challenging practice during sleep involves taking control of your actions in your dreams, or taking control of your running while dreaming. How do you do that? With lots of practice. Remember the time you realized you were dreaming while you were really dreaming? At some time, it happens to everyone. The next time it happens, look at your surroundings and focus. Start by locating and staring at your hands. Once you realize you are dreaming, you can take control of that dream. You can climb a three hundred foot redwood or swim with Orcas in the arctic, or you can run a sub-four minute mile. This practice can enable you to take psychological control of your running by constantly visualizing success and positive results. This can result in the ultimate relaxation and psychological edge.

The practice of controlling your dreams is extremely difficult and some will say impossible. Carlos Castaneda claimed it is not only possible but also liberating and life expanding when achieved. Do you believe in the eternal testament to the transforming power of our dreams? Castaneda said you can perfect skills in your dreams and it will carry over into your waking life.

# TWENTY-SIX

## Cockiness

*"I have been described as confident, cocky or arrogant. I'll take the first one. My confidence is knowing I have probably trained harder than anyone I'm going to run against."*

–Michael Johnson

Confidence is great. Cockiness is just plain wrong.

Beware of smack or trash talking. No one likes a big mouth. At times, as Muhammad Ali and Joe Namath so ably demonstrated, trash talking can be effective, but it's usually a loser's game that may come back to haunt you. Imagine barking at a rival, "Today ain't your day, jack wipe," and it inspires him to hand you your ass.

The law on cockiness states: "Never give the enemy extra ammunition." Many runners run on hate and anger. Why give it to them? Examine the story of Harold Abraham in *Chariots of Fire*. Also, never gloat after you beat a rival, you may have to race him again.

I ran on the cockiest team in the history of Los Angeles, and even we rarely tossed out insults *before* the race. Our most blatant transgression was to perform our notorious "Granada Hills stare-down" at the starting line. Prior to the gun, the seven of us would jog along the starting line and stare at the other team(s). Sometimes we were ignored. Usually they would smile or look away. Maybe a seed of doubt was planted. Other times the "stare" would elicit profanity or a shove. Once a runner from University High School marched up to me after a race and shouted, "I beat your ass. You didn't intimidate me with your stare." It was sweet when I replied, "I beat everyone else on your team and I was our fourth man."

During the race all bets are off. My teammates and I returned every profanity and shove double on the course. Though I still don't recommend the role of instigator, be prepared to fiercely defend yourself and your teammates. Bump, jostle, push, elbow, crowd, stare or swear whenever it is required. Use a forearm to make your point. Get in their face. Never, I repeat, never back down. Don't concern yourself with retribution after the race. Most runners are too tired to fight. Plus, if they're worth their salt, your teammates will back you up.

I'm a big fan of reconciliation. No need to maintain an enemy. Win or lose, always apologize for any misunderstanding. A gentleman is always magnanimous in victory as well as defeat. Never patronize, that's a sure way to piss someone off. Don't be a rotten sport. Show class. Outwardly, be a gracious loser, but on the inside plot mayhem and revenge.

In my junior track season, I ran the varsity 1320 (three lapper) with enormous desire and confidence. Early in the year my main goal was to beat Tab Roberts, a senior from Taft High School whom I had beaten in cross country, but who was the defending league champion in the 1320. Tab Roberts' track reputation preceded him and should have earned my respect, but I was a cocky little bugger and thought it best to hold every opponent in contempt.

During the first three weeks of the season, Roberts ran faster times, until I had a breakout performance against Cleveland. Through the runner grapevine, I heard Roberts had scoffed at my new time and did not consider me a threat. Our meet with Taft was in two weeks. Needless to say, I made certain my race preparations were impeccable. When we arrived at Taft, I learned Roberts was going to run the mile that day instead of the 1320.

To make an ugly story short, I confronted Roberts and made it clear that today was the day to back up any remarks. He claimed the mile was his race and he had nothing to prove to me, which was true. I never called him chicken, as some witnesses insisted later, but I did impress upon him to race or shut his big mouth. I must have struck a nerve. When the first call for the 1320 was announced, Roberts began his warm-ups, much too early for the mile.

"Get ready for an ass whipping, son," Rick Downs, another Taft miler said to me. I grinned at him, but the reality of the challenge, anticipated by both teams, was rather unnerving. I was determined to crush him, but the seeds of fear and doubt had been firmly planted.

The gun sounded. Tab ran smoothly and with intelligence, ignoring a Granada rabbit who was supposed to pull him out too fast. On the second lap, he surged to the lead. I went with him, stride for stride on his right shoulder, and was undaunted though a little more respectful. On gun lap, my signature surge off the first curve worked to perfection and I grabbed the lead down the back straightaway, while every athlete on the track hurled insults and obscenities at the opposing runner. Even the shot putters and high jumpers got into the action. Coming out of the final curve, I five-quick-stepped and attacked the finish line. I owned Mr. Tab Roberts, until five yards to go. He passed and beat me by .2 second. Not only did I have to endure the hoots and taunts from the bleachers, but also the Taft runners appeared from all sides and dished out the punishment. "That's gotta sting, jerk off," and "Don't you hate when you screw up like that?" and "You got what you deserved, big mouth." It wasn't pretty. The defeat was stunning and my humiliation complete. If it weren't for my Granada teammates, I might have shed crocodile tears. But my teammates pushed and shoved their way across the track, brought me water and my sweats, and barked, "Back off" to any Taft runner who looked in our direction.

Later, Mike Lampson advised there was no shame in getting beat by a senior defending league champion by .2 second. When I admitted I was more embarrassed because of my deplorable mouth, Lampson said wisely, "Then learn from it." He added, "Damn, that was the most exciting race of the season."

So I learned a severe lesson in Braggadocio 101. My philosophy on the big mouth was established on that day. I can live with defeat, but the embarrassment caused by my big mouth still lingers forty years later.

# TWENTY-SEVEN

## Weather

*"There is no such thing as bad weather,
just soft people."*
                    –Bill Bowerman

You don't beat weather. You endure weather until it beats the other guy. Use weather as an ally. If you make weather the enemy, it will destroy you. Making weather an ally takes severe mental discipline and training, so the weak need not apply. I detested hot weather. My running performance seemed to crumble in heat and shine in cold. I longed for cold days. Cold weather was a huge psychological boost and I maximized it. Cold pumped me up. When it was cold I was convinced it was going to be my day, regardless of the course or opponents.

Performing well in cold was not a difficult trick. A difficult trick was to make the dreaded hot weather an ally. I was always concerned that heat would cause my performance to suffer, until I decided to make a change. This was not accomplished overnight. Do not expect it to be easy.

First, I had to reassure myself that nobody else liked hot days. If they claimed to like it hot, they were lying. True, there is always some rogue who may actually prefer the heat, but the vast majority of runners who claim not to be bothered by it are lying. I refused to let their lies intimidate me.

Obviously, everyone has to deal with conditions on a hot day. We all wipe our butts the same way. Since no one enjoys heat, it can be used to your advantage. Do you really believe there is a runner sitting under the bleachers before a two-mile race in 104 degrees heat thinking, "I love this shit, and today I kick ass."

Though hot weather sucks, don't let it psyche you out. Everyone else has to run in it. This might be a good time to bring up the point of *not* avoiding lethal weather during workouts. Run in the rain and run in the wind. At times, it may be a good idea to run during the hottest part of the day. Running in the early morning or evening to escape the heat does no good when it comes time to race in the heat. Do not flinch. You may not like the heat, but if you have trained hot you are ready to race hot. Use this knowledge and experience to raise your confidence and develop a mental advantage.

Use tricks to form your alliance with heat. Try short interval work in the heat. Despite popular opinion, if you hydrate yourself properly and listen to your body you will not die. Take breaks in the shade and cool down. If you train in the best conditions, it only seems natural the worst conditions will seem worse. Hot will become your ally because you know hot is kicking everyone else's ass. Everyone is suffering. If hot weather does not destroy you, it will make you stronger and become your ally.

On another note, wind is part of the weather. I ran in the San Fernando Valley, which had the

Santa Ana's, San Gabriel's and Santa Susana's among several others. Ninety percent of the time, when I walked out my door to go to school I was slapped in the face by a strong wind that had the ability to come at you from every direction. In cross country we would sail down a switchback only to make the turn and be stood straight up by the wind. In track, one curve was heavenly while the other was like running into Dr. Lecter in a scene from *Silence of the Lambs*. Adjusting to the wind was crucial to successful running in the San Fernando Valley. Lean forward, lower the head, shorten the stride and pump the arms. Hopefully your weight training will come to your aid. The ability to combat the wind must be honed in practice. Short sprints can be arranged so you run directly into the wind. Turn and jog with the wind to recover. During a race you must concentrate on recovering before your next battle with the wind.

# TWENTY-EIGHT

## Cramps and Pain

*"To a runner, a side cramp is like a car
alarm. It signifies something is wrong, but
you ignore it until it goes away."*
                                        −Unknown

My popularity will drop dramatically
following this next statement: Cramps and pain
don't make a runner quit. Every runner will
experience side or leg cramps accompanied by pain.
It's part of the territory. But never should a cramp
or pain cause you to quit. During my career, I
probably used a cramp or pain as an excuse, which
is my point. Cramps and pain are weary excuses
that no one wants to hear. Excuses are like big butts,
everybody's got one. Slowing down because of a
cramp translates into lack of guts. Pain will always
be part of the equation. Running is about pain and
your reaction to pain.

Injuries don't make you slow down either. If
the injury is that bad you shouldn't be running.

In seven years of cross country and track, I
experienced every type of cramp in the
encyclopedia of cramps, but I never experienced a
cramp serious enough to slow me down. Oh, it
might not have been pleasant. Long distance
running is always sure to be an ordeal. Quite

painful, too. Side cramps will feel like knife wounds while calf cramps can make you feel hobbled. But all they signify is pain. Pain is my point. An experienced runner must learn to endure pain.

When I was coaching cross country at Lake Weir High School in Candler, Florida, many times a key runner, lagging far behind his expected position, would pass me on the sidelines and croak "cramp," as though that was the universal explanation that should immediately elicit sympathy. I came dangerously close to tossing my hat in his face and shouting, "Run with it, you little punk." However, my coaching philosophy always emphasized the positive. A look of disappointment was my only luxury/weapon to motivate rather than destroy the delicate teen psyche. But the cry of "cramp" by a star runner in a big race is a sissy excuse no coach should have to endure. Try to imagine the reaction of coach Giles Godfrey if I yelled "cramp" at the bottom of Pukes Peak with a league championship on the line. I understand hurt, and I know it hurts, but it's only another hurt in a long line of hurts.

Runners with a low threshold for pain need not apply. Runners must learn to live with pain and make pain their ally. When you run twelve 440's under sixty seconds, you will experience pain. Pain will become part of your routine and state of mind. You can overcome pain by training with pain and learning to ignore it. Ignoring pain is part of the razors and psychological toughness that separates great runners from good runners. It's not talent or natural ability that causes some runners to always seem to find a way to perform well, especially when the pack is loaded with well-trained runners who have tons of talent and natural ability. It is the mental toughness that pain can and will be endured, even accepted. Pain can be another ally to the determined runner. While every runner will experience pain, it's how the runner reacts to the pain that makes the difference.

# TWENTY-NINE

## Sickness

*"If the challenge of running was truly ninety percent mental, we would be watching Steven Hawking chase down Einstein's 5K record."*

—Unknown

Don't run sick, period. A simple but powerful cold, if not attended to immediately, can set a runner back two weeks. The flu is much worse. Once I attempted to run with the flu. The first half of the race felt remarkably loose and competitive, the second half resembled the rowing scene in *Ben-Hur*.

Running sick is not worth it. It demonstrates stupidity, not guts. You will invariably feel miserable and run a sub-par race. Why put yourself in the position to be beat by rivals who should not beat you?

Take extra good care of yourself when you are sick. Minimize the damage and get well. Hot baths, good food and vitamins, liquids and tons of rest are what you need. Tone down the training so you don't make yourself sicker.

# THIRTY

## Form

*"If the hill has its own name, then it's probably a pretty tough hill."*
—Marty Stern

Good form is pretty, but not necessary. Good form can economize energy, improve mechanics and make you look swell, but don't be obsessed by it. If you have it, exploit it. If not, live with it. I'll take an ounce of guts over ten pounds of good form any day, especially in cross country.

Running is not ballet or a mystical art form. It is the most basic and beautiful athletic activity on planet Earth, bar none. It is a natural condition requiring no special equipment except shoes, shorts and a path. Runners don't need to look pretty. Running is much more akin to torture than art; it is the Inquisition of sports. Running requires more courage, guts and desire than style.

In a cross country race against Hancock College on our home course, there was a runner from England with a sub-four-minute mile under his belt. Though we were running a four-mile race, it was still exciting to be in a race with a sub-four miler. As their team of eighteen warmed up on the infield, my California Lutheran teammates and I entertained ourselves by trying to guess who was the big man. Narrowing it down, I had definitely ruled out a certain geek with choppy strides, flailing arms and suspect arm strength. He looked like Peter Pan attempting to fly.

During the race, I ran just behind the lead pack from Hancock. At the three-mile mark we approached the Eiger, a treacherous hill that had the letters CLU emblazoned on its slope with large white painted stones. The hill was so steep that runners had to gear down to six-inch strides to reach the top. I practiced every day on the Eiger. Coach Nelson was quoted several times in the school newspaper saying, "When Kent gets to the hills, he walks away." When I reached the Eiger, I passed the last Hancock runner and walked away. On a curve just past the top, coaches, managers, parents and my Dad stood next to their cars shouting out times and encouragement. I looked at Nelson and said, "I'm dead. How far back is the nearest guy?" I wanted to coast. Nelson replied, "Fifty yards in front." In front, I thought? You're kidding. When I came out of the curve, I saw the lead runner. I'm certain you have already figured out he had choppy strides, flailing arms and looked like he was trying to fly off to Never Never Land.

He pummeled me that day. But I looked pretty.

# THIRTY-ONE

## Relaxation

*"If you went for a run today and didn't sacrifice anything, congratulations, you just jogged."*
—Unknown

Coach Pat Connolly preached relaxation. You must learn to relax in a race by learning to relax during workouts. Train to relax. While training, concentrate on relaxation, especially during your speed work. Shake out your hands and shoulders; drop your arms occasionally and shake; twist your neck and keep your head down with your weight shifted forward. During workouts, take relaxation breaks. Breathe deeply and shake out. Lie on your back and get the legs in the air. Shake. Lift one leg at a time a few inches off the ground and shake the ankles, shins and thighs. On your feet, lift one leg at a time and shake. Work on your hands, arms, neck and shoulders. Perform this ritual in the shade, if possible.

While training to relax be sure to pay homage to the Bear. The Bear is the entity that pounces on your back near the end of a race and tightens up your entire body, which makes shifting gears and sprinting miserable if not impossible. Some runners call it "butt-lock." The Bear feels like two hundred pounds and will ruin your finish unless you train to relax. The Bear is not a friend or ally, but he is not necessarily caused by fatigue. The Bear is caused by stress, anticipation and tightness that is part of the territory at the end of a race. By practicing the relaxation techniques described above, during workouts and races, you can eliminate or minimize your bouts with the Bear.

Many runners don't take breaks during workouts. They think it's not a real workout if there are continual breaks to relax and recover. Wrong. Running a straight sixteen miles is good for endurance, but little else. I recommend a long leisurely run on the day after tough races. Otherwise, the competitive runner must develop more creative ways to train. Breaks add to the quality of the training and will yield better results. Breaks help the relaxation and recovery process, which in turn help the next interval to be more effective. Breaks are also important for endurance. I truly believe that to get your heart rate going, slow it down, and then get it going again, over and over, is better for endurance than a long unbroken run, and it is better for relaxation.

For example, when running twelve miles, don't just stride through it. Run the first two miles leisurely in order to warm up. Stop. Shake your arms and legs. Lie on your back and get your legs into the air. Shake out and rid your legs of the lactic acid. Catch your breath and bring your heart rate down. Feel the first sweat. Then run five miles at a medium speed. Don't be afraid to open your stride and push it. Result: your lazy workout becomes a quality workout because your endurance is increased by the acceleration in speed. Stop. Repeat the relaxation routine standing and on your back. Recover. Then run two miles at a fast pace. Hurt yourself and leave it on the course. Stop. Get on your back and rest. You are finished. Jog the final three miles as a cool down. Relax.

# THIRTY-TWO

## The Tape

*"In the first half of the race, don't be an idiot. In the second half, don't be a wimp."*
–Scott Douglas

Brothers-in-arms often speak of the tape in hushed reverence. The magical tape. It's only a lousy piece of string or ribbon strung across the finish line during gun lap, but it awaits the lunging chest or hand of the victor.

To break the tape is an indefinable feeling that transcends description and borders on orgasm. It's the peak of competition in an instant. Fleeting. All the training and effort builds to the moment you lean into the tape. It is life in the extreme present. Then it's gone.

Since the tape is pure joy, when the finish is too close to call you may want to take matters in hand. Hurl yourself at the tape and prepare for a tumble on the track. Opportunities to use this perilous tip will be rare and, of course, extreme. It is not recommended for edging someone out for 197th place. But when the scenario is opportune and important, the option is to sacrifice the body with scrapes and cherries by lunging at the tape and nipping the competition.

I did it three times, only once successfully. Ironically, I was successful on my first attempt and it was spontaneous. Leaping at the tape is not something that should be planned. I thought I was successful on my second try, but the judge shook his head. On my third try I didn't even make it across the finish line. I lunged too early and bonked my head on the track's cement rim. For a moment I saw two lightening bolts. Teammates ran over to help me and I was disqualified. My lone success wasn't even for a win. I was battling for third place in the mile, and it was the last qualifying place for the L.A. City Finals. Also, it was against two runners, not just one. One runner had a slight lead and the other was gaining quickly. I dove at the tape and slid three yards on my chest. The one who had been in the lead made his case with the judges loud and clear. I sat on the track dazed and confused. Both runners circled me and kept asking, "Who got third, who got third?" as if I knew. When an official finally pointed at me, both runners stormed off in a huff and left me on the ground.

# THIRTY-THREE

## Shedding the Sweats and Putting on the Spikes

*"The gun goes off and everything changes...the world changes...and nothing else matters."*

—PattiSue Plumer

To many runners, the shedding of the sweats and putting on the spikes before a race is mindless drudgery. To the true believer, it is a spiritual act.

Always wear sweats during warm-ups before a race, even in the heat. In extreme heat wear only the bottoms. For the ritual to work its magic, it is important to practice proper timing. Never begin the ritual too soon.

Warm up in workout shoes and sweats. If you put on the spikes at the perfect moment, it can be a huge psychological lift. Remember: any psychological lift, no matter how seemingly trivial, is significant. The trick is to devise a dozen or more small psychological lifts where the effect will be cumulative, hence advantageous. The devising will take time and experience to refine. Begin with the sweats and spikes.

If you've never thought about the joy of shedding the sweats and putting on the spikes, it's time to give it serious consideration. Try it. Many cross country races are not conducive to spikes because of pavement, so you will have to settle for going from your old warm-up shoes to your race shoes. Other cross country races and track, however, are ideal. Always have a pair of shoes for racing only. That will make putting them on more special and effective.

Okay, complete your warm-ups. Minutes before the starting gun, begin the ritual. Sit near the starting line and put on the spikes or race shoes. Notice the lightness in your feet. Always double knot the laces. Stand up. Pull one knee up to your chest and shake the ankle. Repeat with the other leg. Remove the top sweat. Then peel the bottoms from your legs and hand the sweats to a buddy. The air on your sweaty legs will feel invigorating. Jog to the starting line.

"Now you are READY TO RUMBLE."

# THIRTY-FOUR

## The Surge

*"I love running cross country. On a track I feel like a hamster."*
–Robin Williams

Train to surge during a race. Train for several surges, if necessary. A surge is a temporary increase in pace in order to catch up with, exhaust, or break contact with a rival. It is followed by a return to pace, and recovery. Obviously a surge can be very painful. Recovery is the key. The surge is different from the five-quick-steps because the surge lasts longer and the acceleration doesn't need to be as quick.

Two major points to surge mastery:

1) You must train in order for the surge to become second nature. Only through difficult and choreographed workout sessions will the surge become a comfortable move. It will never be pleasant, but it can be mastered. Practice running a two-mile at an easy pace. On laps three and six, surge to medium pace. Then on laps four and seven return to the easy pace and concentrate on recovery. Practice a mile run with a third lap surge or an 880 with a third 220 surge. Practice hills with a surge half way to the top, and then recover on the other side.

2) You must develop the guts to initiate the surge in a race. Naturally this will be a tough assignment, because when it comes time to use a surge you will probably feel like crap. Physically it can be accomplished because you've put in the training. Mentally it will feel like swimming up class IV rapids. But think how the other guy feels. I've been on the receiving end of several well-planned surges and it hurt like hell. I delivered a few too. Nobody said it would be easy, but it will be well worth it.

The greatest surge of my career took place during a meaningless practice run. The surge was not only perfectly crafted, but it was perpetrated against my varsity teammates near the end of the season when everyone was in top condition. It occurred on a Wednesday afternoon when the team was supposed to be resting for a Thursday meet. We went on a leisurely six-mile loop up Zelzah to a green water tank, and then down a pleasantly flat trail that ran along a creek. It was a crisp November day. Because of a long team meeting, we got a late start and reached the gate that marked the entrance to the creek trail just as the sun was setting. We stopped at the gate to relax and shake out. After a few minutes, Chuck Franklin said, "I gotta get back," and hopped over the gate. His brother Greg followed on his heels. Tom Horton, Mike Lampson, Alan Silver, Mike Baker and I answered the challenge. There was something about the air, sound of crickets, fading light and smell of sage that inspired me. We chased the Franklins for a mile and a half at race speed. There was a point on the trail where we had to cross the twelve-foot-wide creek.

Since no one liked to get his feet wet, we usually eased up to time our leap. Instead of stutter stepping, I took the lead by splashing straight across the creek. I opened up a gap by storming up the little hill that climbed out of the pass, and surged down the power line road to the high school. Only Lampson stayed close, but even he gave up after we reached Zelzah.

I didn't win the race the next day. I finished third. I checked the newspapers, but nothing was mentioned about my victory on the creek trail.

# THIRTY-FIVE

## Don't Turn Around

*"Don't look back. Something might
be gaining on you."*
                                    –Satchel Paige

Never turn around during a race to check on the competition. It wastes energy, knocks you off stride and looks foolish.

If you want to know where the competition is–listen. There are few things as satisfying as listening to the clicks of an opponent's spikes fade into oblivion, or as fearful as listening to those same clicks quickly approaching. Use your ears. My rule of thumb: if you can't hear them, don't worry about them. If you can't hear them, they have lost contact. If you can hear them, there's no need to turn around because they'll be in your face.

One big reason I frown on turning around is that if the competition is not on your heels there is a natural tendency to ease up. While that may be relatively harmless in a particular race, easing up because no one is on your shoulder could become a dangerous habit that no runner can afford. If the competition makes a surge, there can be a tendency to tighten up or panic.

This strategy may not satisfy everyone. I admit I was obsessed during my career to know precisely where the enemy was lurking at all times. For those who can't stand not knowing, simply place a teammate in a strategic spot on the track or course (more than one, if you wish) with instructions to tell you who is nearby and how they are holding up. You won't knock yourself off stride or look like a worrisome dork.

Final tip: develop peripheral vision so that a slight turn of the head, especially on the turns, will enable you to check out positions and movements.

# THIRTY-SIX

## Remoras and Saint Bernards

*"The competition is against the little voice inside you that wants to quit."*
–George Sheehan

Though this tactic has been ridiculed for its lack of creativity and individualism, I used it successfully in eighty percent of my cross country races. I especially recommend it for occasions when you're competing in a large, definitive meet and your performance is crucial to the team's success. It's called remora running.

A remora is a little fish that attaches itself to a shark. In remora running you attach yourself to a good runner (known as the shark) and do not let go. Run on their shoulder or, if you prefer, directly behind them. This tactic can accomplish a number of goals. If you attach yourself to the right shark, it can boost your confidence and take you to the brink of a great race. Or it can get you through a tough race and even pull you up several places or more.

Simply put, remora running is choosing the right shark and latching on like a barnacle. Never latch onto an inferior runner, unless you are only trying to finish. Unlike bicycle racing, where the drafts can pull you along, the benefits of remora running are more psychological. You still have to do the running; you're just getting a little assistance. You don't even need to think much, other than hanging on and not letting go. In fact the strategy is more effective if you don't think. Stare at the shark's back or feet and sing your song. Eliminate all other thoughts or distractions. Go to your place.

Remora running can improve your position, keep you up with the leaders, bring down your time and boost your confidence. Unfortunately, it does have its limitations. If it becomes habitual, individual wins may be sacrificed. Usually, with remora running, there is little intention of beating the shark because the shark is your savior and you are grateful for being able to hang with the shark. If you remora run with the full intention of keeping up and perhaps challenging the shark, then we are talking about a different game.

Remora running has turned mediocre runners into very good runners. It may be a dead end for the very good runner unless it evolves into a strategy to take down the shark.

A supplement to remora running is the Saint Bernard. If you are totally wasted, dead in the water with no gas, butt locked and quitting, class # 1, is lurking in the back of your brain…hook up with a Saint Bernard. A Saint Bernard is a runner who unwittingly comes to your rescue.

In the midst of your death rattle, latch onto a runner who is passing you, and with a final display of guts and determination allow the Saint Bernard to drag you to the finish line. Hypnotize yourself, stare at the back or feet and hum your special song. Do whatever it takes to force the pain to retreat and allow you to survive.

Latching onto a Saint Bernard is different than remora running because with a Saint Bernard you are only trying to get off the course or track with a finish instead of a quit.

# THIRTY-SEVEN

## Learn to Run Slow

*"I always loved running...it was*
*something you could do by yourself, and*
*under your own power. You could go in any*
*direction, fast or slow as you wanted,*
*fighting the wind if you felt like it, seeking*
*out new sights just on the strength of your*
*feet and courage of your lungs."*
—Jesse Owens

You must learn to run slow. Is that a contradiction to everything else I've been saying? Not if we're talking about training.

When I was a coach at Lake Weir High School, I'd have my cross country team run out to a small pond about a mile from the school. At the pond we would stretch and discuss the day's workout. The run to the pond was supposed to be a slow warm-up. I insisted they jog to the pond. Of course, what did they do? They raced each other to the pond and would be lying down out of breath by the time I arrived. It got so bad I had to force them to run behind me on the way to the pond. They despised running behind me, but they had no idea of the importance of learning to run slow.

Jogging is the critical link that connects the workout. Jogging slow is an art form. To run slow is not only necessary for the warm-ups and warm-downs, it is crucial to the recovery process between intervals. If you jog barely faster than a walk, and shake out, it keeps the muscles warm and loose during recovery and increases endurance.

Most runners jog and warm-up too fast. By racing to the pond, my team expended valuable energy before the actual workout began. Each part of the workout has a specific purpose. The run to the pond was a warm-up. The warm-up is supposed to prepare the body for the strenuous training of the day with as little stress as possible.

After the workout, the warm-down has its job too. When I'd instruct my team to run slowly back to school, they would once again gallop back, screaming and yelling like a pack of Irish Setters. They would screw up the entire purpose of the warm-down and finish their workout with stressed muscles. The purpose of the warm-down is to allow the stretched and fatigued muscles to recover in order to reduce cramping, soreness and potential injury.

Learning to run slow can take interval training to the next level. As the season begins, runners should walk and shake out between intervals in order to recover. As the season progresses, the walking can be replaced with jogging...very slow jogging. I call this recovery jogging. With short steps and shakeouts, breathing and heart rate will recover. This will improve endurance. To jog instead of walk will maintain muscle elasticity and allow the next phase of the workout to proceed smoothly.

Suggested workout:

For interval work, run five 880's under 2:20. After a good warm-up, run the first 880. Then jog a slow 330. Run the next 880. Repeat until finished. With a slow, proper jog as your recovery time between each interval, the benefits of the workout will be heightened.

# THIRTY-EIGHT

## Defense

*"Kick asphalt!"*
–Unknown

High school and college cross country races often become slugfests and barroom brawls. Non-runners will probably scoff, but they have no clue what it's like to set off with 300 runners and within a quarter of a mile have a wide stretch of course turn into a path. Rough physical contact mixed with flying spikes is common. I have been spiked on the toe, ankle, shin and even my hand. I have also been pushed, slapped, elbowed and spit on. Don't feel sorry for me, I have committed my share of offenses and then some. Trust me when I say danger lurks on the course. Track is usually more civilized because of the limited numbers, and the fact that the oval is entirely in plain view.

However, in the 1984 L.A. Olympics, America's distance sweetheart Mary Decker discovered the track could also be a war zone. Mary Decker was the world's best middle distance runner and one of the fiercest competitors on the planet. Midway through the 3,000 meters, a seventeen-year-old South African illegally cut in front of Decker and caused her to trip and tumble onto the infield. Observation and a good stiff arm from

Decker would have prevented the incident. Because of the illegal move on the part of the South African, no official would have disqualified Decker. Decker later admitted she tripped because she was inexperienced with running in crowds. Lesson learned.

Don't be afraid to use your hands for defense. In fact, keep them in front of you while running in crowds. Run defensively and expect contact. When large numbers of runners take off from a starting line, every conceivable type of contact is possible. During my high school career, it was rumored certain L.A. teams carried razor blades to slice the backs of arms in case of contact. I suspect that was an embellishment, but often rumors like that have a basis in truth and will instill fear. At the start of a race, dust can be like an Iraqi sand storm, and runners will weave and bump blindly. Pay attention.

Do not be a bully, but don't take any crap either. Stand up for your rights. One of those rights is to have the opportunity to compete and perform to your best ability without being physically intimidated. Think of yourself as a football running back with a good straight arm.

In the 1964 L.A. City Prelims, a Belmont runner attempted to squeeze past me on the inside, using his hands and fingernails to poke me out of his way. I almost let him get away with it until he called me *puta*, which in Spanish means "you're not a cool guy." My combative juices were aroused. It was my left elbow that caught him under the jaw, clicking his teeth and forcing him to stumble off the course. I finished 5th and he was 8th. He was also waiting for me at our school bus with a group of his *amigos*. Nothing much happened, but it can be a mean business.

Try to avoid the main pack in big races. It may hurt going out a little more quickly, but not as much as picking your way through a hostile crowd in a dust bowl. Run wide on the curves to avoid contact on the inside. Speed up or maneuver if a box appears. The box is when several runners surround you and won't let you get out. A box can beat you as well as any opponent. Many boxes are carefully plotted with extreme prejudice.     Three Biola runners boxed me for three hundred yards in the mile. Though I managed to break out in the final one hundred yards, their big kick artist made quick work of me. I had beaten him in a previous race with a well planned surge. I was livid over the incident, but wiser. Forget tit for tat, just prepare for the tat. Do not acquire vicious habits, but don't tolerate them either. It serves no purpose to complain about enemy tactics. Be prepared.

# THIRTY-NINE

## Be a Good Sport

*"I think sportsmanship is knowing that it's
a game, that we are only as good as our
opponents, and whether you win or lose,
to always give 100%."*
                                        –Sue Wicks

No matter the outcome, no matter what is said before or during a race, and no matter what your emotional state of mind is after a race, you must always demonstrate class and be a good sport. Be noble and be a man. Dr. Julius Erving, one of the finest competitors in the solar system, said something to the effect that a true competitor should never boast in victory nor hang his head in defeat. Make this your mantra.

Though you should always strive to do your best, using every weapon in the arsenal, when it's all over and in the books it is time to stand tall and shake hands. Never gloat or rant in public. Greet victory or disappointment with dignity–there will always be another day. No matter how bad it hurts or how good it feels, mill around the finish line and congratulate the other runners. Be sincere. Some think it is easy to be gracious in victory but impossible in defeat. I disagree. It was much more difficult for me to hold the gushing to a minimum after a win. But you should never gush or gloat after a good race. It's classless and only serves as ammunition in a future race.

In victory, seek out the vanquished, and with no patronizing grin shake hands and say, "Tough race." The defeated are crushed and disappointed. Never throw salt into the wound. Act gracious. The race is over and it is time to demonstrate self-worth.

In defeat, plot revenge; it's an excellent motivator. But do not destroy the moment for someone else with petty or boorish behavior. Many opponents will exhibit poor sportsmanship and/or condescension. You must display finer qualities. As you look back on your sporting days, you don't want to be ashamed or see a John McEnroe throwing tantrums. That image will last forever and be an insult to your sport. Remember: it *is* how you play the game.

Special reminder: seek out the opposing coach and shake his hand too.

# FORTY

## The Lead

*"To move into the lead means making an act requiring fierceness and confidence...and all discretion is thrown to the wind."*
–Roger Bannister

I never enjoyed the lead. Some runners excel in the lead and are comfortable setting the pace. My style of racing would never tolerate the lead for seven laps in a two-mile with three to four guys salivating on my shoulder. I liked to do the salivating. I needed to observe the competition, which is difficult to do when you're in front of them. I liked to make surprise moves, which is difficult to do when they are watching. On the other hand, my hero Steve Prefontaine demanded the lead and would often run away from the competition in the first few laps of the 5,000. I could never mirror my hero. I preferred to hang on a shoulder and wait for my opportunity. Obviously both strategies have advantages and disadvantages. It is up to the individual to decide which strategy fits his or her style, sometimes race to race.

Some runners are addicted to the lead. They do well by establishing the pace and pressuring the other runners to run their race. It's a tough task to lead a pack of good runners from start to finish, but it happens all the time. Paul Burch won twelve straight junior varsity cross country races, including the L.A. City Finals, and not once did he relinquish the lead.

My philosophy was to run with the pack and never lose contact (two to six yards) or get left behind during the surges. The lead is important only at the finish line. Move up when it feels comfortable and recover from surges while hanging on to a shoulder. Most of the races I won, I had the lead for less that 400 yards. That was enough.

At times, opponents would try to force the lead on me with a slow pace. The only times I would fall for that trick were when I knew someone in the pack had a dynamite kick. Otherwise, if they wanted to turn a two-mile race into an 880 that was fine with me. If the pace is too slow and you are forced to take the lead, run like the mob is after you and make Mr. Sprinter keep up. Hopefully your pace will diminish his kick.

# FORTY-ONE

## Quick Tips

*"You play to win the game...HELLO."*
–Herm Edwards


Quick Tip # 1 – Do a minimum of one cross-training activity in order to increase your endurance. I suggest swimming, bicycling, aerobics or hitting the bag.

Quick Tip # 2 – Pump the weights.

Quick Tip # 3 – Don't forget to train for the five-quick-steps. You must be able to shift gears quickly and decisively.

Quick Tip # 4 – The only way to beat hills is to train hills. Unless it's Pikes Peak, always try to sprint up hills in workouts and races. It's a natural inclination for runners to simply want to survive a hill. You must use hills to destroy other runners. Remember: no one likes to speed up at the top of a hill.

Quick Tip # 5 – As you peak during the season, train to run relaxed. Lean forward and drop your hands to your sides. Shake out. Hum your secret song or go to your special place. Drop the shoulders and rotate your head. Allow your cheeks to jiggle.

Quick tip # 6 – Jim Evans taught me this mini-trick by kicking my ass. If you are caught in a potential sprint to the finish with a runner you know will give you a race, gasp out something like, "I'm finished," or "I've gotta stop," or "Go on without me." Then let up slightly to demonstrate you are really suffering, all the while gathering strength for a final five-quick-steps. With any luck, this mini-trick will lull your opponent into a false sense of security and he may let up and not expect a fight. This will be your opening. Reload and do your five-quick-steps. You may catch him napping and steal the momentum.

Quick Tip # 7 – This is war. You must fight and run like there is no tomorrow.

# FORTY-TWO

## News Clipping Syndrome

*"You're allowed to suck in a race
only if you make certain everyone
else sucks worse."*
                    –Unknown

"Don't come to the starting line with your
news clippings pinned to the front of your jersey,"
warned Coach Giles Godfrey. In other words, don't
expect press accounts of previous races or weekly
lists of top times to compel your next opponent to
roll over at the starting line. Don't expect your
reputation to frighten them, either. Previous results
or times don't mean crap in the next race. Beware.
If you haven't faced a runner, then you haven't
beaten that runner. Headlines and good times can
cause overconfidence and that can be dangerous.

On the flip side of the coin, never allow a
rival's news clippings, reputation or times
intimidate you. At the starting line, previous results
are history.

In tenth grade, I allowed two senior San
Fernando runners to whip my ass in the 880 because
they had both placed in the top five in the league
finals the year before and both had slightly better
times. During the race, I had an excellent
opportunity to make a strong move and take control

of the race, but was paralyzed by my perception of their superior times and reputations. Instead, I ran their race and got beat.

"What happened to YOU?" Godfrey asked after the race.

I was incredulous. "They were too good," I stammered.

"Bullshit," he roared. "You lost that race before the gun sounded. You could have taken them both on the third curve and made a race of it. I saw you were itching to pour it on and make a move. But you were so intimidated by their 'big reps' you turned into a chickenshit."

That stung because it was true. Never allow news clippings, reputations or times to beat you. Demand to be beaten on the track or course. Also, never expect the other runner to roll over because of your previous times or the news clippings pinned to your jersey.

# FORTY-THREE

## Drink Tons of Water
## and Eat Honey

*"Warning: the surgeon general didn't say
anything about smoking the competition."*
–Unknown

Throughout your entire career and for the
rest of your life, drink tons of water. Never allow
yourself to become dehydrated. Don't use salt
tablets. In the heat, salt tablets have a tendency to
cause nausea. Nothing, and I repeat, nothing
replaces H20. Drink water whenever you think
about it, and then some. Not one sport drink is
better than water; it's all marketing hogwash. 10K's
and under, there is no need for water during the
race. Anything above a 10K will require a re-
hydration agenda.

Drink tons of water after the race in order to
recover, re-hydrate and reduce the possibility of
cramps. Ignore advice to go easy on the water after
a race. I would drink until I heard water jiggling in
my stomach.

Side tip: Honey is probably the best natural
energizer on the planet. It goes straight to the blood
stream. Try a good dose of honey fifteen minutes
before a race for a natural surge of energy.

# FORTY-FOUR

## The Legendary Second Wind: Fact or Fiction?

*"You will come to your peak slower than many and you will be running last. But when it is really important to be running first, you will be passing them."*

—Arthur Lydiard

It's a fact. Most experts believe a two or three-mile race is too short to achieve the legendary second wind. They could be right, but I disagree. I will admit the times when I was absolutely certain I had achieved a second wind occurred during workouts of six or more miles, and it was euphoric. There is a moment when you actually believe you can run fast forever. Doesn't last forever, perhaps a mile or two, but you will remember the feeling forever.

Here's how it usually happens (and it might occur one out of twenty times). The first three to four miles feel fine, the next two begin to hurt, and then it becomes deathly...until you push beyond the threshold and experience a magical boost in energy and lucidity. Nirvana.

I've also experienced something akin to the legendary second wind in a two-mile race. Maybe it should be called the "mini" second wind. First three laps feel good. The next two begin to hurt, and the final three can become the Death March to Bataan, unless you push beyond the pain threshold and discover new life. Rather than a genuine second wind, you experience a "mini" second wind. The final lap and a half can become mini-Nirvana. It can be achieved, I promise. Maybe not very often. But by using proper breathing, relaxation and mental focus, you can will yourself into another level of energy that will result in euphoria. Whether it is more psychological than physical I cannot say.

Beware: achieving a second wind may lead to severe running addiction. It may become your new religion.

# FORTY-FIVE

## Tough Lessons

*"It's supposed to be hard. If it wasn't hard, everyone would do it. The hard is what makes it great."*
—Tom Hanks in
*A League of Their Own*

The first major crisis of my running career occurred mid-way through the tenth grade cross country season. I had emerged as the second man, often threatening the number one, on a powerhouse team that swept most opponents and eventually grabbed the West Valley League and Los Angeles City titles.

In the first five races I finished second place, and only Canoga Park's Richard Little averted five Granada Hills shutouts by placing third. I must admit I was satisfied to be second man. There was quite a bit of pressure on number one, and it would have taken a monumental effort to unseat him. Second man gave me enormous prestige without the huge expectations. I was in a comfort zone that was dangerous, and I should have noticed a red flag.

Our sixth race arrived with some major competition from Chatsworth. Les Myers was supposed to challenge our number one for the league individual title and since no other runner from another team had challenged me, I was a bit startled by the competition. Fear got the best of me and I ran with hesitancy. I dropped the ball mentally. Not only did I get beat by Myers, but our third man, Alan Silver, also beat me.

As my fourth place finish became apparent, I wanted to shout obscenities and shed crocodile tears. It was at that moment our fourth man, Mike Newman, stepped up to the plate and taught me a valuable lesson. I was sick with jealousy and self-pity, and wanted Alan Silver to die. Mike Newman, running on my shoulder, pointed out that Alan was on the brink of beating Myers in the final one hundred yards.

"Take him, Silver," he shouted. "Take him down."

At first, due to my ego, I refused to join in. But Newman continued to cheer and shamed me. Finally, I recovered my voice.

"You got him, Alan," I croaked. "He's all yours."

Surprisingly, I meant it. Damned if Alan Silver didn't beat Myers, absolving me of my sins and petty jealousy. It hurt in a hundred different ways, including the fact Alan had accomplished what I was supposed to have accomplished. Of course, Mike Newman was a man and I was a little boy. From that moment on I made it a habit to shout words of encouragement to all my teammates on the turns and switchbacks, regardless of who had the lead. I did it with purpose and sincerity. I believed it was important for the team and the development of my character. Oh, I still wanted to destroy Alan Silver and everyone else, but I also wanted my teammates to perform well because they had earned my respect and support. My teammates responded with like behavior and a new Granada Hills tradition was born. Every race thereafter we all shouted encouragement to each other. That team lost in the City prelims, but stormed back to win the finals.

There was a team perception that I had started the tradition. I never discouraged that belief, but it was not true. Mike Newman deserved all the credit. Also, a rivalry with Alan Silver began that was to last my entire high school career. It was a rivalry of mutual respect. As the Cheyenne dog soldiers believed, "You are only as strong as your enemy."

The moral of this story is that teammates are your brothers-in-arms. In races, a simple tap on the back, arm or elbow can spark a teammate to keep up the pace. Words will work even better. Sometimes a stern look or threat works best. Runners must be conscious of the mental and physical state of their teammates during a race. Remember: a cross country team is only as good as its fifth man. In fact, great cross country teams win with their fourth, fifth and sixth men.

When Granada Hills had a big showdown with Birmingham High School during my senior varsity campaign, Birmingham took first and second. I had shut down mentally and was destined to finish out of the top ten. That is, until Tom Horton sacrificed a possible third place and came to my rescue. Tom Horton literally dragged me back into the race and jolted me out of my funk. We placed fifth and sixth, beating their third man and securing the win. Without Tom's sacrifice we might have lost that race. On that day Tom Horton beat Birmingham, and THAT is how great cross country teams operate. Only one runner wins individual championships in cross country. Coaches, staff, parents, friends and seven runners win team championships.

With good teammates, it's more than just the races. It's the workouts too. But it's still more. It's the talking before a race to pump each other up. It's the nightly phone conversations that provide the support and confidence that every runner needs. It's the friendships that will last a lifetime. Mike Newman and Tom Horton introduced me to the unselfish attitude that wins team championships.

# FORTY-SIX

## To Be Beat or to Be Broken

*"Mental toughness is a muscle that needs
exercise just like the muscles of the body."*
–Lynn Jennings

No matter who you are, you will be beaten many times and by many people during your career. Olympic champions get beat. Don't dwell on it. There is no dishonor in a beating. How you respond to the beating, during and after the race, is much more important.

Getting beat leaves a sour taste, but it happens to the best runners. During a race, when a beating becomes apparent, do you give up and/or lose confidence? Following the beating, are you convinced you can never beat the other runner no matter how hard you train? If so, you may have been broken. Defeats should motivate a runner to train harder and become more determined, but getting broken can cause severe psychological damage. Never give in to defeat. No matter how badly you are beaten or how bad it feels, finish the race as strongly as possible and plot revenge. Hold your head up high. Never allow yourself to be broken. I know that's easier said than done.

In one of my grandest races, I was destroyed but not broken. It was the West Valley League

Finals in the mile. This was an individual championship that I wanted desperately and was even the slight favorite. It was a weeklong media-hyped confrontation that may have been the highlight of my high school career. I was a senior, my rival a junior. We were both unbeaten. He was the younger brother of a Valley "legend." I had just beaten the defending league champion in the preliminaries. I had the best time by over two seconds. Also, I wasn't afraid. I was in the best shape of my life and had the proper attitude. This was my event and my year.

On the third lap, I initiated my signature surge. It worked to perfection and I opened up a six to seven yard gap. But on the back straightaway of the gun lap, he took me by surprise with an astonishing burst of speed. Though I was more than a little stunned, I fought back and managed to remain on his heels around the final curve. I maintained my stride and form. I dug deep into the vault and exploded with a marvelous kick that fell short, 4:22.8 to 4:24.4. Although my defeat stung badly, I was strangely pleased with my performance. For once in my career, I didn't quit when I was getting beat. I went for the victory. I didn't settle for second place, I only finished in second place. I was not broken.

So I learned. I trained harder, plotted new strategy and sharpened my razors. He beat me in the City Finals too. But I know he beat me straight up. I never quit in a race against him. Defeat can be your ally because it can make you tougher and more determined. Belief after a victory is simple. Belief after a defeat is a victory.

# FORTY-SEVEN

## Living with It for the Rest of Your Life

*"When it's pouring rain, and you're bowling along through the wet, there's satisfaction in knowing you're out there and others aren't."*
            —Peter Snell

Like it or not, and whether you realize it or not, there won't be any more high school or college races after high school and college. These races will echo permanently in the universal record book known as your memory.

For the high school and college runner, no matter your condition or cramps, mental or physical wounds, weather, illness, constipation, gas, heartburn or any other miserable excuse you can muster, you will live with the results for the rest of your life. It's almost unfair. There will be times down the road of life when you will relive the races and dwell on the "what ifs." The good races will taste like Champagne and the bad ones vinegar. And there's nothing you can do about it. Trust me on this. I'd give my left testicle to run the final 1,000 yards of just one of my races that tastes like vinegar. Please let me have the final 1,000 yards of my senior cross country City Finals, not in any better shape or possessing any advantage other than the knowledge of what I know now–that I will have to live with the results for the rest of my life. That jolt of reality should do me just fine. Alas, it will never happen.

Use this knowledge as motivation. Though we can't always be at our best, and maybe our bad races are part of the cycle all runners must endure, if I knew then what I know now about living with those disappointments for the rest of my life, I would have challenged grim death in order to improve the results. But there are no second chances, and that is the point. Use my experience and disappointments to formulate a psychological edge. Dig deep; all runners can go a bit deeper, if not a lot deeper. Do it because, whatever the results, you will have to live with it for the rest of your life. In a perfect world, I would be awarded a second chance. Then I would spit, claw and kill myself to do better because thirty-seven years is a long time to dwell on a shitty race.

Run every race with this attitude. Use your future suffering to your advantage on every race day.

# FORTY-EIGHT

## Always Fight Back

*"Our greatest glory was not in never falling, but in rising when we fell."*
—Vince Lombardi

For three grueling years of Los Angeles high school cross country, myself and ten runners from each of the sixty-seven high schools in three divisions (tenth grade, junior varsity and varsity), which multiplies into an impressive two thousand and ten runners, were subjected to the tyrannical persecution and whims of the Old Starter.

Lawrence Olivier could have picked up dramatic pointers from the Old Starter. His lengthy, inane instructions before each race continued *ad nauseam*:

"Keep your toes behind the line, boys."

"Remember to follow the chalked arrows."

"Don't box up at the chute."

"Don't grab onto the turning poles."

"You'll be disqualified for pushing, elbowing or punching."

"Listen carefully to my instructions."

"We'll get you going real soon, boys."

Few listened to a word he said. Please shut your yap and shoot the gun.

Every single race was the same. Introduction of race officials and sponsors, announcements about the concession stand, and warnings to spectators to stay off the course. Each announcement was painfully long, all performed with a bullhorn in one hand and starting gun in the other. He was a big, burley fellow with a red beard and gray tousled hair. He always wore baggy Levis, T-shirt under an open red flannel shirt, and black combat boots. He was Ernest Hemingway playing Forrest Gump. At dual meets, league finals, City Quarters, City Prelims and City Finals, the Old Starter started every race. Also he was an intimidator. He delighted in picking on individuals who may have been talking or appearing to not pay attention. "Excuse me, South Gate number two, I guess one hundred and eighty of us will have to wait until you stop yapping with your boyfriend." This was *his* show.

When the fluff was finally completed, the Old Starter strode down the starting line, with exaggerated histrionics, and swept back all toes planted on the line with his black combat boots. "Behind the line, boys." Upon reaching his starter position, he would stare at us for a moment, and then ask, "Any questions?" Of course, there were none. Then he would bark, "Last chance to tie your shoelaces, boys."

His final instructions: "I'm going to give you two commands, take your mark and runners set. Then I'll fire the gun." Long pause. "Okay, here we go." Whistles and more whistles. "Timers and judges ready?"

"Take your mark." At least thirty seconds elapsed. "Runners set." Kapow.

My senior year, during the 1966 City Prelims, I was personally humiliated by the Old Starter. During his instructions, he caught me flipping off a runner from Palisades. His stare was so intimidating it shattered my concentration. When he growled, "Runners set," I leaned forward a fraction too far and was slightly off balance. He sensed my mistake and waited patiently. As I stumbled over the chalk, he fired the gun and one hundred and eighty runners bolted off the line. Whistles and several gunshots followed. The bullhorn barked, "Recall, boys, recall. Return to the starting line." When order was finally restored and everyone was back in position on the starting line, the Old Starter chortled, "Granada Hills number six, false start. If a second false occurs, Granada Hills will be disqualified." Then he winked at me.

The incident demanded retribution.

One week later at the Los Angeles City Finals, following the same pointless instructions and drivel, when the Old Starter got to the part where he asked if there were any questions, I stepped forward and raised my hand.

"Yes, son," the Old Starter said over the bullhorn. "Granada Hills number six has a question."

Everyone on the Pierce College course turned toward Granada Hills. We had drawn lane one and were boxed between a patch of mud and seventeen other schools. I looked the Old Starter in the eye. After a significant pause, I bellowed, "LAST CHANCE TO TIE YOUR SHOELACES, ASSHOLES!"

Always fight back.

# EPILOGUE

*"May the road rise to meet you, may the wind be always at your back."*
                    –Irish Proverb

At the end of my 1966 senior cross country campaign at Granada Hills High School in Los Angeles, I knocked on the door of Coach Giles Godfrey's gymnasium office and peeked in the window. The room was cluttered with trophies, including a new one for the 1966 L.A. varsity title.

"Come in, Kent," he growled from behind his desk, "and shut the damn door."

I sat down and waited for him to speak.

He looked me over and smiled. "Thank you for growing up and leading this team to the championship. I'm real proud of you, son."

My face reddened. "The team really pulled it together."

"I spoke with Coach Chambers at Valley State. He's going to offer you a full ride."

I stood up. "Coach," I said, extending my hand, "it's been an honor."

We shook hands.

He said, "Now get the hell out of my office before I put my foot up your ass."

# The Runner

On a flat road runs the well-train'd runner,
He is lean and sinewy with muscular legs,
He is thinly clothed, he leans forward as he runs,
With lightly closed fist and arms partially rais'd

- **Walt Whitman**

# Recommended Reading

1. *Once a Runner*, John L. Parker, Jr.
2. *Pre: The Story of America's Greatest Running Legend, Steve Prefontaine*, Tom Jordan
3. *Bowerman and the Men of Oregon: The Story of Oregon's Legendary Coach and Nike's Co-Founder*, Kenny Moore
4. *Runner's World Guide to Cross-Training*, Matt Fitzgerald
5. *The Runner's Yoga Book: A Balanced Approach to Fitness*, Jean Couch
6. *Coaching Cross Country Successfully*, Joe Newton
7. *Gerry Lindgren's Book on Running*, Gerry Lindgren
8. *Running and Being: The Total Experience*, George Sheehan
9. *Running to the Top*, Arthur Lydiard
10. *Born to Run: A Hidden Tribe, Superathletes, and the Greatest Race the World Has Never Seen*, Christopher McDougall

# Acknowledgments

I want to thank Keith Baumann, Terry McCray, Karen Morrison, Rob Burgess, Todd Carstenn, Axel Kent, Carlin Burgess, Kristen Moreau and Shelby Blaes for support and encouragement.

Special thanks to my editor Daniel Barth for insight, guidance and "The Old Runner." This book was huffing and puffing on the track until you snatched the relay baton.

# About the Author

G. Kent lives in the wilds of the Ocala National Forest in North Florida. He was born and raised in Los Angeles. He is also the author of a novel, *Bandits on the Rim* (Tenacity Press, 2012). For more information contact kentib@earthlink.net.

Back cover photo: G. Kent competing for California Lutheran College, 1969.